MATH FOR SMARTY PANTS

Marilyn Burns

illustrated by Martha Weston

What are "smarty pants" anyway?

SCHOLASTIC INC.
New York Toronto London Auckland Sydney

To find the year this book was written, just add any row, column, or diagonal in the square below, or the four corners plus the middle number.

390	403	386	394	408
396	405	392	400	388
402	385	398	407	389
409	391	399	387	395
384	397	406	393	401

ISBN 0-590-48940-2

Copyright © 1982 by the Yolla Bolly Press.
All rights reserved.
Published by Scholastic Inc., 555 Broadway, New York, NY 10012, by arrangement with Little, Brown and Company (Inc.)

12 11 10 9 8 7 6 5 4 3 2 1   5 6 7 8 9/9 0/0

Printed in the U.S.A.   14

First Scholastic printing, January 1995

This book is dedicated
to anyone who likes the idea—
even a little bit.

What's in this book?

GETTING STARTED

What does it mean to be a mathematical smarty pants? It sounds like it means being smart in math. And it does. But that only helps if you understand what it really means to be smart in math. And that's not so simple to explain because being smart in math can mean several things, and different things.

Here's an example. There are some kids who are whizzes at dealing with numbers. They do arithmetic fast, really fast. Ask them which is a better buy, two for a nickel or three for a dime, and they've figured it out in a jiffy. (Do you know?) And not only do they know for sure whether ½ or ⅓ is larger, they can tell you fractions that fit in between those two, lots of them. (Can you?) They never seem to forget where the decimal point goes in a problem, or how many times a number goes into another. Are these kids smart in math? In a way, yes. Being smart with numbers is one way to be smart in math. But it's not the only way.

Then there are the kids who are great with shapes, who can "see" things easily in their heads. When a certain kind of problem comes along, it's just their cup of tea. For example, they can tell if a particular shape, such as this one,

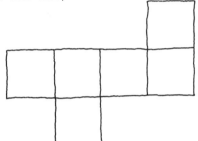

will fold up into a cube, without having to cut it out and test it. (Will it?) There may not even be numbers in the kinds of problems these kids are good at and like to do, but with anything geometric, it's a cinch. Are these kids smart in math? Yes, they're smart, in a different way than the number whizzes are.

Some kids are good at strategy games and puzzles that don't have much to do with either arithmetic or shapes, but have more to do with thinking logically to figure things out. Give them puzzles, and they're the first to find a solution. Play a game of giant tic-tac-toe with them, one with a board like this one,

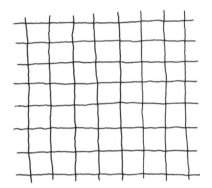

where you need four in a row to win, and they are tough to beat. Really tough.

For some kids, being fast in math is important. They like to get the right answers, in a hurry, and then get on to the next problem. Not so for others. Other kids tend to work a long time on problems, never seeming to be in a rush, and often are just as interested in seeing if there are other solutions to the same problem. Neither one of these kids is necessarily more of a mathematical smarty pants than the other.

Are You a Math Smarty Pants?

You may be wondering if you qualify as a mathematical smarty pants. You're not alone. Lots of kids wonder about that. What's important for you to realize is that mathematical smarty pants come in many types. The truth is this: You're not born being a math smarty pants—it is something you learn. The real trick to being a math smarty pants is believing that math makes sense, or *can* make sense if you put your mind to it. If you believe that, or are willing to believe it, even just a little bit, then this book can help. Believing takes practice, and the best kind of practice is math practice. There's plenty of that in this book. You can be a mathematical smarty pants if you really want to. It's up to you.

I'm BOOTS. I just got this calculator for my birthday. I used to borrow my parents' calculator, but then I left it on by mistake and it got all weird, making mistakes in arithmetic. I thought that was pretty funny, but my parents didn't laugh at all. Now I have my own.

Hi, I'm T.J. This is my friend; we call him SPEEDO. He and I are really different kinds of kids. Speedo is always jumping around. He can't even stay still long enough to introduce himself. But I'm kind of calm and even. I'm not in a hurry all the time like he is. You know, I think that Speedo had better slow down, or he'll burn himself out before he ever gets to be a grownup.

A Special Note to the Math Hater

Maybe you hate math. Really hate it. You have no idea whether it's better to buy two for a nickel or three for a dime, or whether any shape will fold into a cube, and you're not sure you even care. What you're wondering is: How come I've read this far in this book anyway?

Consider this: The reason you're reading this book right now is that there's a part of you, a mere fractional part (as a math smarty pants might describe it), that doesn't feel quite right about hating math. And you'd like a second chance to set the matter straight.

Some people think that being good in math is just getting the right answers to problems; they think you either know how or you don't. That's just not true. The first step in getting good in math is believing there is a difference between not being able to figure out a problem and not figuring it out right away. When a problem seems hard, instead of thinking "I can't do this," think "I just haven't solved this problem yet." You don't need to rush in mathematics!

If you want a second chance, give this book a try. You may learn you're smarter in math than you think!

PART 1
Arithmetic with a Twist

13

Arithmetic is the part of mathematics that has to do with numbers — adding columns of numbers, doing division problems, multiplying, and subtracting. Sometimes those numbers are fractions or decimals. You've heard all this before. It may even be old hat to you. The arithmetic in this chapter, however, may not always seem like the arithmetic you're used to. But if you look carefully at all the stories and problems, you can find the arithmetic lurking in them. It's kind of sneaky sometimes, but it's there.

The $1 Word Search

"Excellent" is a $1 word, mathematically speaking. So is "discipline," which is what you'll need to find more of these wonders. To find them give each letter a cent value: a = 1 cent, b = 2 cents, c = 3 cents, and so on up to z = 26 cents. Then add the value of each letter in a word. Check for yourself to see that "excellent" and "discipline" really are $1 words. Now it's up to you. How about your first name? Is it worth $1? ("Suzanne" and "Kristin" are. So are "Henrietta" and "Christian.")

To help in your search for more of these valuable words, here are some hints. There is a Halloween word that is worth $1. (Nope, it's not "Halloween"; that's worth only 95 cents.) There's a Thanksgiving $1 word, as well as one astrological sign and one U.S. coin. There are at least two U.S. cities—one is in Wisconsin, and the other is in both Oregon and Maine.

There's a beverage that is illegal for kids to drink that's worth $1, though it sometimes costs more than that to buy it in restaurants and bars. There are several animals at the zoo that are $1 words, and one underwater creature. There's a number less than 100 that's worth $1, as well as something you wear to keep your hands warm in the winter.

At this time more than 200 $1 words have been discovered by addition-loving kids from all over the United States. How about having a $1 word contest at your next party? And if you read carefully through this book, you'll find $1 sentences stuck in from time to time—sentences in which every word is worth $1.00!

Mathematical Stunt Flying

Mathematicians have their own version of stunt flying. They use numbers instead of airplanes. (Wouldn't you know it!) They get their thrills from numerical loopings and from discovering patterns while they're doing their tricks. One person's pattern is another's loop-the-loop.

Looping — 4-2-1-4-2-1-4-2-1-4.

NUMBER **1.** Start with any number you like and follow these rules. If the number you start with is even, divide it in half. If it's odd, multiply it by 3, then add 1. Whatever answer you get, apply one of these rules to it again. And do that over and over again—that's the looping part.

Here's a sample. Start with 10. It's even, so take half. That gives you 5. That's odd, so multiply it by 3 and add 1: $(5 \times 3) + 1 = 16$. Back to even, so take half and get 8. Half again gives you 4. Half again gets you to 2, and half again gives you 1. Since 1 is odd, multiply by 3 and add 1 to get 4. Half of 4 gives you 2, and half of that gets you back to 1. You're in a loop now and will be forever if you keep at it.

Try the same procedure with 30 and see if what you get matches this: 30, 15, 46, 23, 70, 35, 106, 53, 160, 80, 40, 20, 10, 5, 16, 8, 4, 2, 1, 4, 2, 1.

Try a few more. If you start with 88, you'll have 17 steps to go before you hit 1. If you start with 27, it takes 109

steps! With a calculator, you should be able to poke right along; without one, you'll still get there—it will just take a while longer.

Here goes **3**. It's **odd**, so I'll multiply it by 3, which makes 9. Add 1, that gives me **10**. That's even, so I

divide it in half and get **5**. That's **odd**, so I multiply it by 3, which

Hmm.... Looks familiar already.

makes 15, plus 1 is **16**. Back to even so half of

This system for looping interests mathematicians. In fact, it has interested some mathematicians so much that they've tried starting with every number from 1 to 1,000. Every one loops into that 4—2—1 pattern at the end.

Mathematicians are never satisfied, and the question they have is this: Will every number loop into that pattern? Well, there's no telling. It's not possible to figure out a proof. A proof is an explanation that convinces everyone that something is true without their having to try it over and over again. As clever as mathematicians are, not one of them has come up with a proof that looping back to 4—2—1 will always happen. No one has found a number that doesn't work, but no one has been able to prove that *any* number will work. It just goes to show that mathematicians don't know everything.

Looping 8–9–7–6–3–9–2–1–3–4–7– NUMBER 2.

For this numerical stunt, you start with any two numbers from 0 to 9 and follow this rule: Add the two numbers and write down just the digit that is in the ones place. Here's an example: Suppose you start with 8 and 9. Adding them gives you 17. Keep just the 7, which is in the ones place. So now you have 8—9—7. Add the last two numbers, the 9 and the 7. That gives 16; keep just the 6, then you have 8—9—7—6. Keep going, adding the last two numbers in the series each time, keeping only the digit in the ones place. Do this until you get 8 and 9 again. Then the loop starts all over. The 8—9 pattern has twelve numbers in the loop before it repeats.

If going around in a numerical circle appeals to you, you may have the makings of a terrific mathematician. Hang in there. But beware. If you start with the same two numbers, but in the opposite order, and follow the same rule: 9—8—7—5, and so on, it will take 60 numbers before it starts to repeat! Don't tackle that one unless you're sure you have the time. For a quickie, start with 2 and 6.

Here are the kinds of questions mathematicians ask about an exploration such as this one: How many different possible pairs of numbers are there to start with? (It's okay to start with two numbers that are the same.) What's the shortest loop you can find? What's the longest loop? Is there a pattern of odds and evens in the loop?

Looping NUMBER 3.

This is a numerical looping that also uses words. You start with any number, 39, for example. Write it as a word: thirty-nine. Then continue as shown.

Start with any number	39
Write it as a word	thirty-nine
Count the letters	10
Write that as a word	ten
Count the letters	3
Write that as a word	three
Count the letters	5
Write that as a word	five
Count the letters	4
Write that as a word	four
Count the letters	4

You'll get 4 forever and ever now. As a matter of mathematical fact, you'll get to 4, no matter what number you start with originally. Try a different number and see. Convince yourself with some examples, then see if you can figure out why you'll always get to four.

Dealing in Wheeling

Have you figured out the problem T.J. presented to Billy and Speedo? If not, here's a hint. Try solving this one first; it's an identical problem: A kid bought a tape recorder for $40, then she sold it for $50; she later bought a record player for $60, then she sold it for $70.

Now you may think this isn't much of a hint. As a matter of fact, you may think the two problems are not identical at all. Well, they are. Don't let the bicycle part in T.J.'s version throw you off the track. You have to see beyond that to get into the mathematics of this.

This problem has caused fierce arguments in Berea, Ohio, in Smithtown, New York, and in Mill Valley, California. So beware if you ask for help.

Consecutive numbers are numbers in order...

...like when I pile the cards on top of the aces in solitaire.

The Pattern of Consecutive Sums

Looking for patterns is a mathematician's idea of a swell time. It's like hunting for treasure that you know is there, if you can just unearth it. Sometimes patterns appear in the most obvious places. Even in easy addition.

Here's an addition investigation that is a problem with some interesting patterns lurking in it. This investigation has to do with writing numbers as the sum of consecutive numbers. Consecutive numbers are numbers that go in order—like 1, 2, 3 or 29, 30, 31, 32 or 745, 746—and don't skip to get from one to the next. So 6, 8, 9 aren't consecutive because the 7 was skipped. And 1, 3, 5, 7 aren't because with them you need to add two to get from one to the next.

Here's a sample of how to write a number as the sum of consecutives: $9 = 4 + 5$. But 9 can also be done another way: $9 = 2 + 3 + 4$.

The number 12 can only be done one way: $12 = 3 + 4 + 5$. The number 15, however, can be written as the sum of consecutive numbers in three different ways: $15 = 1 + 2 + 3 + 4 + 5$, $15 = 7 + 8$, $15 = 4 + 5 + 6$.

Your job in this investigation is to find all the possible ways to write each of the numbers from 1 to 25 as the sum of consecutives, using only whole numbers: 1, 2, 3, 4, and so on. Look for patterns. Which can be written as the sum of only two consecutives? Which can be written as the sum of three consecutive numbers? Four? More? Between 1 and 25 there are five that can't be done at all; what are they and what are their patterns? The patterns can be found everywhere, if you just know how to look.

P.S. The number 315 can be written as the sum of consecutive numbers 11 different ways; 315 is the smallest number with that characteristic.

Answer to *Dealing in Wheeling*:
It comes out $20 ahead.

Chummy Numbers

When two numbers are friends in mathematics, they are called "amicable." Take 220 and 284. There's a pair of very buddy-buddy numbers. You may be wondering why they're so friendly. (I certainly hope you're wondering. Curiosity about such matters is the first step toward becoming chummy with mathematics.)

Well, here's why. The numbers smaller than 220 that divide into it evenly are 1, 2, 4, 5, 10, 11, 20, 22, 44, 55, and 110. And the numbers smaller than 284 that divide into it evenly are 1, 2, 4, 71, and 142.

If you add up each of those strings of numbers, you will find that the divisors of 220 add up to 284, and the divisors of 284 add up to 220. Pretty chummy, wouldn't you say? And definitely unusual.

There aren't many numbers that are such tight friends as these. Maybe that's why numbers such as these were once thought to be mystical.

An Italian named Nicolo Paganini found a pair of amicable numbers when he was just 16 years old—1,184 and 1,210. Doublecheck his work. Do you agree with him? Two other pairs were found in the seventeenth century —17,296 and 18,416, and 9,363,584 and 9,437,056.

Do you have any idea how someone would set out to find a pair of amicable numbers?

21

The Three Little Pig Eyes

Have you heard about the three little pig eyes? These are legendary, mischievous creatures, tricksters really, who are fair in their hearts, but who spend much of their free time playing tricks on people. And they play many tricks since practically all of their time is free time. It's one of the advantages of being a legendary creature.

The magical, mischievous pig eyes are not quite as well known as some other fabled creatures. Or maybe they are just not as popular. Perhaps it's because they have hideous, annoying laughs. They're either laughing at their own jokes, jokes that no one else would think are at all funny, or they're laughing at other people, who weren't even making jokes.

Here's an example of the kind of trick they play, one that they thought was really funny. They played this trick on Sally McCrackin, who didn't think it was funny at all. That's usually the way with their tricks.

Sally McCrackin was walking home from school one day. She had just said goodby to her best friend, Lisa, and was walking the last stretch alone, reaching into her school bag for the sack of peanuts she was saving for this part of the walk. (Sally loves peanuts.) She had the sack in her hand and was about to reach in for her first peanut. Suddenly, from the side of the road, out jumped one of the tricksters with little pig eyes.

"Peanuts, huh!" the trickster cried. "Oh, how I love peanuts," and it grabbed Sally's sack right out of her hand.

"Give me that!" Sally shouted. "You have no business grabbing a kid's sack of peanuts. They're mine, and you'd better give them back to me."

The trickster laughed one of those hideous laughs, and that's when Sally got a little scared.

"You can have a few if you like," she said a little nervously.

"I can have as many as I like," replied the trickster, "but I feel pretty generous today. I'll just take half of them." And it dumped out the peanuts, dividing them into two equal piles. Sally watched, feeling astonished and helpless. It stuffed one pile into its pocket. Then it put the rest back into Sally's sack. "And," the beady-eyed creature said, "I think I'll take just two more from your sack." Which it did, throwing the sack back to Sally, and then disappeared behind a tree.

Sally was stunned. And wouldn't you be? She stood there for a minute, holding her sack, with the ringing of that laughter still in her head. Then she began to walk on again, a bit shaken. What else could she do?

A little farther on, when Sally was feeling a bit better and her heart wasn't pounding so hard and her breathing seemed calmer, she decided to chalk up the experience as one of life's hard knocks. She reached into the sack to cheer herself up with one of the remaining peanuts.

But even before she could eat one peanut, another of the little pig eyes jumped into her path. "Eeeaaahhh!" it screamed. The scream turned into screeching laughter when the little pig eyes grabbed the sack right out of Sally's hand. "I loooooove peanuts."

As you might imagine, Sally was stunned. What an unlucky day this was turning out to be. But, finally, she shook herself into action and spoke with the voice she had learned to use when her dog was misbehaving. "Give me that sack of peanuts *right now,*" she said, stamping her foot.

This made the trickster laugh so hard that tears were pouring out of what seemed like the tiniest eyes Sally had ever seen. "I'll give them to you when I'm ready. Goooood and ready. But first I'll take some for myself, if you please, or even if you don't please. I'll take half, I think." Then this little pig eyes dumped the peanuts out, dividing them into two piles, stuffing one pile into its pocket, and put the rest in Sally's sack. "And," it said, laughing so hard it had to hold its stomach, or what seemed to be its stomach, "I'll take just twooooo more and be on my way." Which it did, leaving Sally's sack on the ground, and disappeared into the field on the side of the road.

Now Sally was a very reasonable person who liked to make sense of things. But this was a tough one to figure. She didn't feel afraid exactly. She felt more startled, like she did when a mouse caught her by surprise or when a snake appeared in the road. These piggy tricksters were very unusual, bizarre even, but they didn't seem dangerous. Just wait until I tell Lisa, she thought, as she picked up her sack. But would Lisa believe this? Was it really happening? Who were these creatures, with their little pig eyes and their grating laughter. They certainly are rude, she thought, whatever they are. And not knowing what else to do, Sally walked on, reaching into her sack for one of the remaining peanuts.

As you may have already guessed, Sally didn't get that peanut out of the sack. Trickster number three popped out. This one was a fast-stepping, finger-snapping weirdo who did not seem to be able to remain still for even an instant. It hopped around Sally, snapping its fingers, clapping its hands, talking as fast as it moved. "Peanuts, peanuts, I love peanuts. And most of all, I love your peanuts. Do not dawdle, my little sweet. Hand over the sack, the entire treat."

This time Sally got mad, really mad. "Don't call me your little sweet. I'm not your little anything, and I know what you want. You want half my pea-nuts, then two more, and I think that's mean. And I think you're weird and ridiculous looking, and you probably have a hideous laugh."

That seemed to be the funniest thing the trickster had ever heard, judging from the way it fell to the ground laughing and shrieking, grabbing the sack at the same time. "You're right, my clever peanut lover," it said, turning somersaults. "Half plus two more, that's for me; a more cooperative Sally there will never be. A pile for me, a pile for you, then I'll reach in your sack and also take two." Off it ran, running with a strange gait, clicking its heels, swinging its arms over its head.

All this was too much for Sally. She had been brave up to this point, but now she'd had too much. She sat down at the side of the road, clutching her sack. She opened it up and looked inside. There were only two peanuts left. Only two peanuts. A little while ago her sack had been full. Sally put her face in her hands and started to cry, loud, jerking, long, hard sobs. Finally she stopped crying, gasping for breath, and reached in her pocket for a handkerchief to dry her eyes. She looked up, and there in front of her were the three creatures, not laughing at all now, but lined up staring at her.

Sally tried staring back at them but could feel herself beginning to cry again. She tried to control herself; she hated having them see how upset they made her. "You're mean!" she said to them, raising her chin a little.

"We're just tricksters," the first one answered.

"Hrrummff," Sally said, still sniffling.

"It was just a trick we played. That's what we do; we play tricks on people," the second one said.

"You took my peanuts, that's what you did," Sally accused.

"We'll give them back to you if that will make you feel better," the third one said.

Sally looked at them suspiciously. "Prove it," she said.

The three huddled together in a group, whispering to each other. Sally sat there, unable to hear what they were saying and very tired of the entire situation. She wanted to get her peanuts back and to go home and forget the whole thing.

The three came out of their huddle.

"We've agreed to return all your pea-nuts to you," the first one said.

"But we have decided that we'll do this only if you can figure out a prob-lem," said the second one.

"Oh, no," Sally said, rolling her eyes. "Now what do you want?"

"Well," the fast-talking third crea-ture said, "playing tricks is our favor-ite thing to do, and we're good at it."

"So I've noticed," Sally commented.

"But," it went on, ignoring her, "sometimes playing tricks isn't very nice, and we know that, so we substi-tute being tricky for playing a trick. We've got a tricky problem for you, and if you can solve it, you'll get every peanut back. Honest."

"Why not just give me the peanuts?" Sally asked. "They are mine, you know."

"We can't do that," the second trick-ster explained. "Since we're trick-sters, we have to have some fun. Being tricky is alllllllmost as much fun as playing tricks."

"Would you like to hear the prob-lem?" the first little pig eyes asked.

"Oh, all right," Sally replied. "What is your tricky problem?"

They answered in unison. "How many peanuts were in your sack when it was full?"

"I don't know," Sally said.

"That's the problem," the first one said, giggling a little.

"You can figure it out. You know we each took half plus two more," the second one said, starting to giggle also.

"And you have two left in the sack," the third one said. And the three of them began rolling on the ground, laughing and laughing.

Sally ignored their laughing and began to think. After a while she got out some paper and a pencil and wrote some figures. Then she collected some pebbles to use as the peanuts. She actually got interested in the problem. And, sure enough, she solved it.

As soon as Sally announced her answer to the three little pig eyes, they emptied their pockets and counted up to see if she was right. She was, and they put all the peanuts back into her sack, gave it to her, and scampered away, laughing as if this were the funniest thing they had ever done.

What answer did Sally come up with?

Like many math problems, this one can be solved in several different ways. It is a tricky problem since it seems as if it has to do with arithmetic, but not the usual arithmetic. It's not a "trick" problem, like the "What's Odd About This?" problem on page 86. Tricky problems are fair and square, but trick problems have a sneaky twist that can stump even the best mathematical thinkers. Discuss this problem with someone else to see if you can find different ways to solve it.

On Which Day of the Week Were You Born?

Even though you were there at the time, you may not know on which day of the week you were born. Your parents may remember; then again they may not. (You never can be sure what grownups will remember.) With some careful mathematics, however, it's possible to figure out on which day you were born. Just follow these directions.

1. Write the last two digits of the year you were born. Call this number A.

2. Divide that number (A) by 4 and drop the remainder if there is one. This answer, without the remainder, is B.

3. Find the number for the month in which you were born in the Table of Months below. Call this number C.

4. On which date of the month were you born? Call this number D.

5. Add the numbers from each of the first four steps: A + B + C + D.

6. Divide the sum you got in step 5 by the number 7. What is the remainder from that division? (It should be a number from 0 to 6.) Find this remainder in the Table of Days. That table tells you on which day of the week you were born.

This method works for any date, as long as it's in the twentieth century. You can't use it to find out days before 1900. It *will* help you find out on which day of the week Halloween or your next birthday will land. In the back of some telephone books there is a perpetual calendar. That calendar will help you check to see if you did your mathematics correctly.

TABLE OF MONTHS	
JANUARY	1 (0 in a leap year)
FEBRUARY	4 (3 in a leap year)
MARCH	4
APRIL	0
MAY	2
JUNE	5
JULY	0
AUGUST	3
SEPTEMBER	6
OCTOBER	1
NOVEMBER	4
DECEMBER	6

TABLE OF DAYS	
SUNDAY	1
MONDAY	2
TUESDAY	3
WEDNESDAY	4
THURSDAY	5
FRIDAY	6
SATURDAY	0

Have you ever heard the Mother Goose rhyme, "Solomon Grundy"? Here's one version of it:

> *Solomon Grundy*
> *Born on Monday*
> *Christened on Tuesday*
> *Married on Wednesday*
> *Took ill on Thursday*
> *Worse on Friday*
> *Died on Saturday*
> *Buried on Sunday*
> *This is the end*
> *Of Solomon Grundy.*

How is that possible? With a bit of logical thinking, it's possible to explain how the life of Solomon Grundy really could have happened as the rhyme says it did. It's surprising how often mathematical thinking is useful.

I wonder if that rhyme has anything to do with years?

Answer to *The Three Little Pig Eyes*:
Silly starfish putt Ed in her back sack.

★ $1 SENTENCE ★

Whenever wizards whistled, elephants spouted.

Incredible Calculators

Have you ever noticed that some people can do arithmetic faster than others can? Sometimes this is because one person has had more practice than another. But some people can do arithmetic computations so incredibly fast that practice doesn't honestly explain their abilities.

Throughout history there have been lightning-fast calculators who could do remarkable arithmetic feats in their heads. Their talents have amazed the slowpokes around them. Thomas Fuller was called the "Virginia Calculator." He was captured and brought to America from Africa as a slave in 1724, when he was only 14 years old. It wasn't until he was 70 that he became well known for his arithmetic talent. He could easily perform feats such as multiplying two nine-digit numbers in his head. Once, when his rare ability was being tested, he was asked to figure out how many seconds there were in the 70 years and 17 days he had been alive. He figured it out in a minute and a half—in his head. The examiners who were testing him figured the answer also—on paper, of course. They got a different answer. But Thomas Fuller was able to show them that they had forgotten about leap years! Thomas Fuller died in 1790 at the age of 80, never having had any formal schooling and without even learning to read or write.

··>⟨<··

Zerah Colburn was the son of a farmer. He was born in Vermont in 1804. His parents never thought he was very bright, but after he had been in school for only a month and a half, they heard him reciting parts of the multiplication tables. His father, curious about his son's interest in multiplication, asked Zerah, "How much is 13 x 97?" "1,261," Zerah answered, as quickly as *you* might give the answer to 3 x 5. Zerah was only six years old at the time. Zerah's father immediately took Zerah out of school and on an exhibition tour with high hopes of earning lots of money by showing off his son's remarkable talent.

"flew around the room like a top, pulling his pantaloons over the tops of his boots, biting his hands, rolling his eyes in their sockets, sometimes smiling and talking, and then seeming to be in agony." In less than one minute, he had come up with the correct answer: 133,491,850,208,566,925,016,658,299,941,-583,225! Truman admitted that he was tired after doing this calculation. Truman never did public exhibitions. He eventually went to college and studied astronomy; but as he got older, he lost some of the amazing abilities he had had when he was young. He died in 1901.

At the age of eight, when Zerah was giving a demonstration of his powers in England, he was asked to compute 8 to the 16th power. That means 8 x 8 x 8 x 8 and so on, multiplying 8 by itself 16 times. He gave the answer, which is 281,474,976,710,656, quickly and easily and brought the astounded audience to tears.

Zerah received his formal education in England. With education, strangely, his calculating abilities decreased. Eventually he returned to the United States, where he tried acting and schoolmastering, becoming a preacher and later a teacher of Greek, Latin, French, Spanish, and English. He wrote his autobiography, explaining some of his calculating methods. Zerah Colburn died in 1840.

.--.=-.=--.

Another calculating prodigy, Truman Henry Safford, was born in 1836, also in Vermont. When he was ten years old, the Reverend H. W. Adam gave him this problem: Multiply in your head 365,365,365,365,365,365 x 365,-365,365,365,365,365. According to Reverend Adam's description, Truman

There have been others with these incredible calculating abilities. If these stories were interesting to you, you may want to find out about other arithmetic prodigies. Ask a librarian for help in finding information about John Wallis; Johann Carl Friedrich Gauss; Andre Marie Ampere; George Parker Bidder, Sr.; George Parker Bidder, Jr.; Johann Martin; Zacharias Dase; Jacques Inaudi; and Shakuntale Devi.

Speedo Multiplication

Some of the people who have been famous calculating whizzes have been able to explain some shortcuts. It's unlikely that you'll be able to match their extraordinary feats, but you can learn some calculating tricks and dazzle your friends and family. You may even dazzle yourself.

Most calculating shortcuts require that you do some mental arithmetic, and often keep some figures in your memory. Here's a speedo way to multiply any number by 11. Try this method to see if you can get good at it and if you like this sort of thing. It may seem complicated to learn, but once you do, it's really fast.

When you multiply a number by 11, using this method, you get your answer one digit at a time, starting in the ones place and moving to the left. Here's an example: 523 x 11.

1. The ones digit of the answer is the same as the ones digit of the number you're multiplying by 11: 3.

2. To get the tens digit of the answer, look at the tens digit in the number: 2. Add that to its right-hand neighbor (the 3 in the ones place): 2 + 3 = 5. That's the tens digit in the answer. Now you have 53.

3. Continue the same way. To find the next digit of the answer, find the digit in the same place in the number and add it to its right-hand neighbor. The answer so far: 753.

4. The farthest left-hand digit in the answer is the left-hand digit in the number. The final answer using this method is 5,753. Do you agree?

1. Here's another example. 145 x 11 — The ones digit in the answer is 5.

2. Now I'll add the 4 to the 5 and get 9 for the tens place. 145 x 11 = 95

3. Now I add the 1 to the 4 and that's 5. 145 x 11 = 595

4. Last of all, the 1 goes in front to finish the answer. 145 x 11 = 1,595 Real speedy!

Write down a few more "times 11" problems, and you'll start to see why this shortcut works.

Sometimes when you add a number to its right-hand neighbor, that sum is more than 9, so you have to carry 1, just like in regular addition. For example, if you use this method to calculate 892 x 11, you'll have to carry 1's.

To multiply by 12, the method is almost the same as for multiplying by 11. The difference is that you double the digit before adding its right-hand neighbor to it (except for the final digit). So to multiply 564 x 12, follow these steps:

1. To get the ones digit, double the ones digit in the number you're multiplying by 12: 8.

2. For the next digit in the answer, take the 6 and double it, then add it to its right-hand neighbor: $12 + 4 = 16$. Write the 6 and carry the 1; now you have 68.

3. For the next digit, take the 5 in the number, double it, then add it to its right-hand neighbor, which is 6: $10 + 6 = 16$. Then add the 1 you carried from the previous addition to get 17. Write the 7 and carry the 1. This gives you 768.

4. The left-hand digit of the answer is the same as the left-hand digit in the problem, but you have to add the 1 you've carried, so it's 6. The final answer is 6,768. Check it.

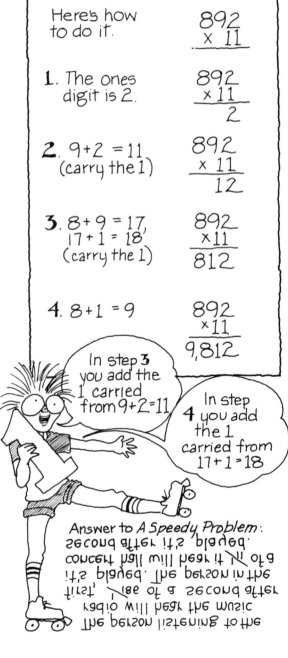

Here's how to do it.

$$\begin{array}{r} 892 \\ \times\ 11 \end{array}$$

1. The ones digit is 2.

$$\begin{array}{r} 892 \\ \times\ 11 \\ \hline 2 \end{array}$$

2. $9 + 2 = 11$ (carry the 1)

$$\begin{array}{r} 892 \\ \times\ 11 \\ \hline 12 \end{array}$$

3. $8 + 9 = 17,$ $17 + 1 = 18,$ (carry the 1)

$$\begin{array}{r} 892 \\ \times\ 11 \\ \hline 812 \end{array}$$

4. $8 + 1 = 9$

$$\begin{array}{r} 892 \\ \times\ 11 \\ \hline 9{,}812 \end{array}$$

In step 3 you add the 1 carried from $9 + 2 = 11$

In step 4 you add the 1 carried from $17 + 1 = 18$

There are tricks for doing other calculations as well. If you are interested, check in the library for books about arithmetic shortcuts.

Answer to *A Speedy Problem*: The person listening to the radio will hear the music first. It's played. The person in the concert hall will hear it a fraction of a second after it's played.

Answer to *The Million-Dollar Giveaway*: Even your *great, great, great, great* Big Gramma milli0n dollars to give away at $50 a month would take 20,000 months!

Upside-Down Riddles

You might think that your calculator can only communicate with numbers. But you can get it to flash words too. Punch in numbers, then turn your calculator upside down to see if you made a word. To get the idea, punch in 3045, turn your calculator upside down, and read SHOE. Try 35009918 and read BIG GOOSE.

Now you add the riddle part. You get a riddle and a clue. Riddle: What do you do in rain puddles? Clue: 15025 x 3. Try it to see if you get the answer SLOSH.

Here are some more. What sound does a turkey make? (189403 x 2 + 3). What surrounds a baby chick before it hatches? (1546686 x 5 + 12563). What kind of pop is good to lick? (53121 ÷ 3).

The Eights Have It

$$9 \times 9 + 7 = 88$$
$$9 \times 98 + 6 = 888$$
$$9 \times 987 + 5 = 8,888$$
$$? = ?$$

Can you continue the pattern?

What Comes Next?

Figure out what's happening here, then see if the pattern continues.

$$1 \times 8 + 1 = 9$$
$$12 \times 8 + 2 = 98$$
$$123 \times 8 + 3 = 987$$
$$1,234 \times 8 + 4 = 9,876$$

These patterns really begin in the good, old multiplication tables. Write down the 8's and the 9's in vertical columns, and you'll see where the fancy patterns get their start.

Divisibility

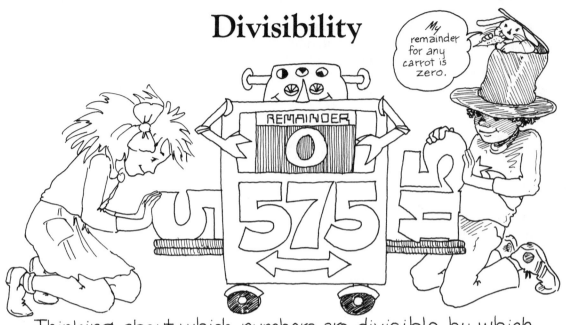

My remainder for any carrot is zero.

Thinking about which numbers are divisible by which others is a topic that interests mathematicians. For one number to be divisible by another means that it can be divided by it with no leftovers; the remainder is zero.

2

For a number to be divisible by 2, for example, it has to be even. Numbers such as 8, 10, 64, and 2,368 are divisible by 2; 5, 67, and 103 aren't. So you can tell whether a number is divisible by 2 just by looking to see if it's even. You don't actually have to do the division.

3

Deciding if a number is divisible by 3, however, isn't so obvious. Take 144, for example. You can't tell just by looking whether 3 will go into 144 with no remainder or not. You could find out by dividing, but there's another way. To test if a number is divisible by 3, add up the digits in the number you're testing. Is that sum divisible by 3? Take 144, for

example: If you add 1 + 4 + 4, you get 9. Since 9 is divisible by 3, so is 144. Not so with 145. If you add 1 + 4 + 5, you get 10, which isn't divisible by 3, so neither is 145. You can check these on your calculator. This test is useful for large numbers such as 273,645. Add the digits: 2 + 7 + 3 + 6 + 4 + 5. The sum is 27. Still not sure? Then add the 2 and the 7. That should convince you.

4

For divisibility by 4, you can test by looking at the last two digits of the number you're testing. If that number is divisible by 4, so is the entire number. This works well for large numbers such as 2,365,716. The last two digits are 16, which is divisible by 4. Check with your calculator to see if the larger number is also.

5

You can go back to the "look" method to test for divisibility by 5. Any number that ends in 0 or 5 is divisible by 5. That's easy.

6

See if you can figure a divisibility test for dividing by 6. Hint: You have to combine two of the tests given so far.

7

A really tricky situation is the test for divisibility by 7. A weird 3—2—1 pattern helps here. For example, to test an enormous number, such as 6,124,314, you have to figure like this: 3 x the ones digit + (2 x the tens digit) - (1 x the hundreds digit) - (3 x the thousands digit) - (2 x the ten thousands digit) + (1 x the hundred thousands digit) + (3 x the millions digit). Try the test on 6,124,314, then check your test by actually dividing it out—with a calculator if you'd like. Then use part of the test to show that 18,102 is divisible by 7. (Watch the + and - signs.)

You might be thinking that it's easier just to divide, rather than go through such a complicated test. Maybe so. But for some people, thinking about the tests is lots more fun than doing the division, with or without a calculator. Some people will spend a long time— once—looking for a shortcut they can use forever.

37

The Calculator Argument

Once upon a time two mathematicians were having a discussion. An argument, really. "Calculators are terrific arithmetic tools," said one of the mathematicians.

"I agree," said the other. (That wasn't what the argument was about.)

The first mathematician went on. "I wonder why they even bother to make kids learn how to do arithmetic with paper and pencil. Why don't all kids just get a calculator along with all their other school supplies?"

"What?" said the second mathematician. That's when the argument started. "That's crazy. Having a calculator to use is a convenience, I agree, but it doesn't replace knowing how to do something on your own."

"Why should kids have to learn how to do something that they never have to do, something that a calculator can always be used for?" the first mathematician answered.

"Why should kids not have the advantage of knowing how to do arithmetic? It would be like having to carry an extra brain around in their pockets. What if they had to do some figuring and didn't have their calculators with them? Or what if the batteries were dead? What about that?" The argument was getting serious.

"No one is ever in that much of a rush. Doing arithmetic is never an emergency situation. Having to wait to get a new battery would seem to take less time than all the time it would take to learn and practice how to do arithmetic. That takes years to do, years that kids could spend doing much more interesting things in math."

"Look," the second mathematician went on, exasperated, "kids need to learn to be self-sufficient, to be able to depend on themselves to do jobs. Using a calculator isn't bad; it just shouldn't be the only way kids can do arithmetic. It just doesn't make sense."

The first mathematician wouldn't budge in the argument. "The calculator is a tool. When you do a job, it makes sense to use the best tool there is to do that job. If you have a pencil sharpener, you don't use a knife to sharpen a pencil. If you're in a hurry, you don't walk; you go by car. You don't walk just because it is the way you always got there, just because that was the way people used to travel."

"Aha!" answered the second mathematician. "Walking is still useful. You knew how to do that before you learned how to drive or ride a bicycle. Just because we have cars, we don't discourage kids from learning how to walk. That's a ridiculous argument."

Their argument went on and on. And on. And to this day, it hasn't been resolved. So kids still are learning how to do arithmetic. And they're also learning how to use calculators. What about you? Which mathematician do you agree with?

Let's just hope they take a break for dinner.

This argument was made up, but it's like those that many grownups are having about what to do with kids and calculators. Probably you don't have a choice; you have to learn how to do arithmetic. That's that. In the meantime, you also can learn to use your calculator. Learning to use a tool is a good idea, and there are lots of chances in this book for you to do just that. Keep an eye out for them.

41

There's more to math than numbers. Lots more. Mathematics has a great deal to do with shapes too. When you study shapes in mathematics, you're studying geometry. This does not mean that you don't have to think about numbers when you're thinking about geometry. But here it's the shape of things that matters most.

It Doesn't Always Look Simple

In mathematics a curve is any continuous line. It can have straight parts, angles, and curvy parts; but as long as you can draw it without lifting your pencil, it's called a curve.

If the curve doesn't ever cross over itself, it's a "simple" curve. If the curve ends up back where you started, it's called a "closed" curve.

There's more. There are simple closed curves. A simple closed curve is made when you get back to your starting place without ever crossing over the line at any point. If you have crossed over somewhere, then it's just a closed curve. It's enough to make you dizzy.

A circle is a simple closed curve. So is a triangle and a square and a pentagon and any polygon, for that matter. What's a polygon? Here we go again. A polygon is a shape made of straight line segments that connect and don't ever cross themselves.

That's enough for now. This stuff could make you crazy.

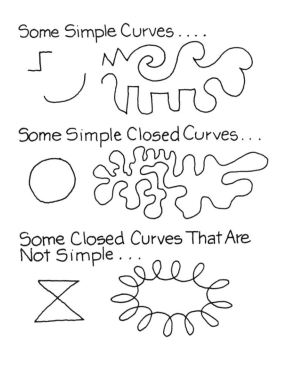

Some Simple Curves . . . .

Some Simple Closed Curves . . .

Some Closed Curves That Are Not Simple . . .

Don't Make a Triangle

This is a two-person game of geometric strategy. You'll each need a pen or pencil— each of you must have a different color. First, trace the six dots as shown here for the playing board.

The way to play the game is to take turns drawing line segments. Each line segment connects two dots. The way to not lose is to avoid drawing three lines in your color that connect to make a triangle. If you do make a triangle in your color, you lose. The way to win is to force your opponent into having to draw a triangle in her color. If someone completes a triangle, but not all three sides are the same color, it doesn't count.

A note: To learn to draw the dots without tracing them from this page, you have to think "hexagon"—a figure with six sides. If you connect each of the six dots shown here to its neighbors, you'll have a hexagon with equal angles and sides of equal length. It's called a "regular hexagon," regular because all the sides and angles are equal. When drawing your own dots, it's not essential that they all be spaced exactly the same distance apart, but it is essential that no three of the dots lie in a straight line. If they did, you would not have a hexagon when you connected the dots. Sketch it to see why.

How many moves would this game take if you wound up connecting every dot with every other dot? How many line segments would that be? Connecting on the outside would give you the six line segments that make the hexagon. Connecting all those on the inside would give you lots more.

If you think that's too much drawing and counting, try thinking about the problem a different way. In mathematics it often helps to solve a problem by first solving a simpler one. Then you make the problem a little more complicated and solve that one. And as you keep doing this, you look for a pattern that will give you the answer to the hard problem, and perhaps to other related problems as well.

Instead of six dots, start with one dot. For one dot there aren't any lines you can draw. Pretty simple, huh?

Okay, now move up to two dots. If you have two dots, there is only one possible line to draw.

What about three dots? If you connect each of them, you have a triangle, and that's that.

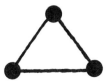

With four dots there are six lines.

Organizing this information makes it easier to examine.

DOTS	LINES
1	0
2	1
3	3
4	6
5	?

Continue the pattern, and use it to help you figure the answer for connecting five dots, six dots, or seven, or ten, or however many you'd like.

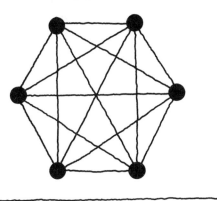

There's More Than One Way to Fold a Cube

If you cut this shape out of heavy paper or cardboard, you can fold it up and tape it into a cube.

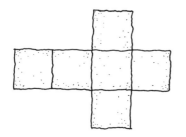

(Try it if you're not sure how it goes.)

Even though a cube has six sides and needs a shape with six squares to make it, the squares don't have to be in the shape shown above. They could be arranged like this instead:

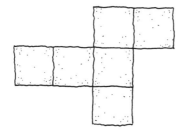

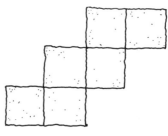

Besides these three arrangements, there are eight more ways to cut out six-square shapes that would fold up into cubes. You just need tape to hold them in shape. Try to find them.

Quick Change

Can you change a regular hexagon into a cube by drawing only three additional line segments?

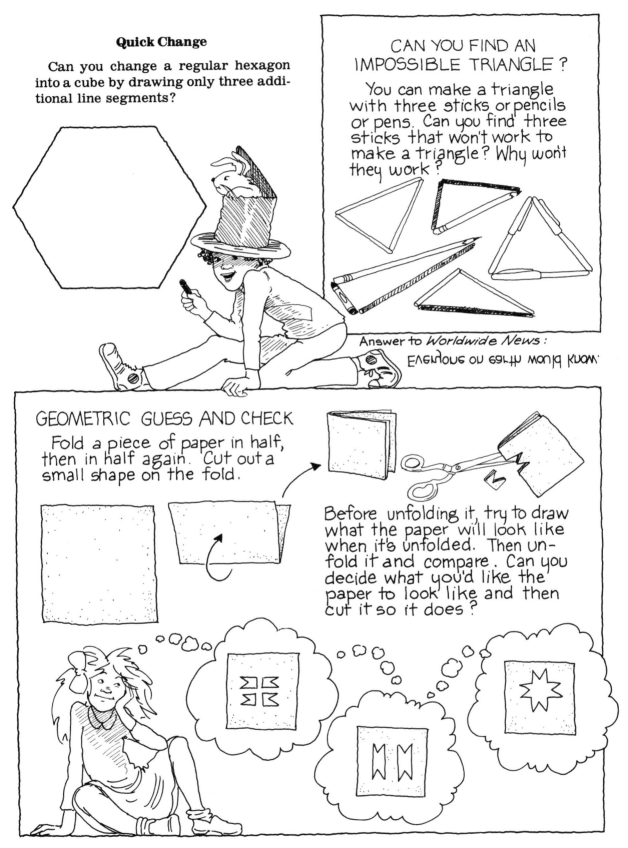

CAN YOU FIND AN IMPOSSIBLE TRIANGLE?

You can make a triangle with three sticks or pencils or pens. Can you find three sticks that won't work to make a triangle? Why won't they work?

Answer to *Worldwide News*:
Everyone on earth would know.

GEOMETRIC GUESS AND CHECK

Fold a piece of paper in half, then in half again. Cut out a small shape on the fold.

Before unfolding it, try to draw what the paper will look like when it's unfolded. Then unfold it and compare. Can you decide what you'd like the paper to look like and then cut it so it does?

The Wobbly Cube

Kim Hick is more of an artist than a mathematician, but he mixes both in his work, which is making stained-glass windows and mirrored shapes with intricate ins and outs of angles. Through his art he makes math that's terrific to look at.

In his work Kim Hick often makes cardboard models of shapes he wants to explore. The exploration is a lot like playing with mathematical figures, and that's how he invented the "wobbly cube," a shape that can lie flat, pop up, and take several shapes in between.

Try making one for yourself.

1. Cut 24 strips of cardboard 1 inch by 4 inches (or 2 ½ centimeters by 10 centimeters).

2. Lay 4 strips in a line, each separated by about the thickness of the cardboard. Run a long piece of tape over them, letting the tape overhang as shown.

3. Fold over the end with the tape overhang as in the drawing. Then fold over the other end. Press down firmly so the tape will stick.

4. Open your "rectangle ring" and reinforce it by taping each hinge on the outside. (*The best way to reinforce a hinge is to have the tape on both sides, directly opposite each other and touching in that little crack between the pieces.*) Then make five more rectangle rings with the rest of the strips. You should have six rings when you're done.

5. Tape four rings together from outside as shown. Then complete your wobbly cube by adding a ring to the top and one to the bottom.
Hint: There's always a way to hold the wobbly cube so the pieces you're taping will lie flat.
   When you have finished, explore the different shapes it can fold into.

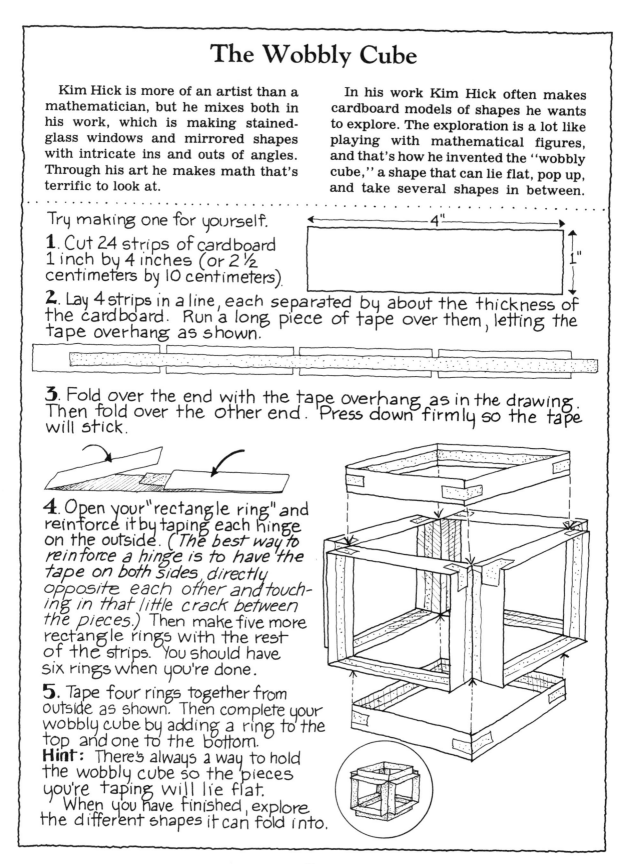

Testing Your Geometry Memory

Remembering shapes in geometry isn't very hard for most people, except perhaps the stop-sign shape. Some people can't remember whether it has six sides or eight. (Do you remember?) Usually shapes are pretty easy.

Give yourself a quickie mental test. Can you picture a circle? A square? A pentagon? If you can, you're ready for the bigtime.

Remembering *sizes* in gemoetry is another story. Not so easy for some. See how you do.

Get a piece of paper and draw each of the following shapes as close to their actual sizes as you remember them. Then get out the objects and see how you did.

★ A **circle** the size of a U.S. quarter

★ A **rectangle** the size of a dollar bill

★ A **triangle** the size that a can opener makes in the top of a can

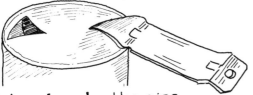

★ A **rectangle** the size of a standard playing card

★ A **square** the size of the end of a stick of butter

★ A **circle** the size of one of the holes on the telephone dial (or a **square** the size of one of the push buttons)

★ A **rectangle** the size of a stick of chewing gum

★ A **circle** the size of the buttons on your shirt or pants

Dinky buttons!

I was right!

How did you do? Try it again in a week or so to see if your memory improves. Is it important to remember sizes anyway?

Answer to *A Fraction Fooler*:
The answer is one-half.

Answer to *Which Is Bigger?*:
one quintillion or 10_{18}
They're both the same—

49

A GEOMETRY RIDDLE

With a geometric stretch of your imagination, can you explain how half of 8 might be 0 or 3?

That probably happens when a pig eye is dividing up peanuts.

No!

Numbers Can Be Square

49

Some numbers are square, and some aren't. If you want to test whether 9 is square, for example, you need to get nine objects. Pennies will work. You can line up nine pennies in rows so that each row has the same number of pennies in it, and together they make a square.

The number 8 isn't square. There's no way to push eight pennies into rows that make a square. It's no go. The number 4 works, however. Prove this to yourself. Then see if you can find other square numbers using this penny method. (You may even be able to talk your parents out of some spare, square change. Tell them there is a mathematical experiment in the works.)

To find square numbers you don't have to have pennies, or any objects at all; you can do it by multiplying. Pick any number and multiply it by itself. Let's take a small number, 3. Multiply 3 by 3 to get 9, which the penny test showed is a square number. Multiply 4 by 4 to get 16, another square number. Test that one with the pennies. Start even smaller, with a 1; 1 x 1 = 1, so 1 is a square number, even though one penny won't show it.

Oh brother, what a square!

17 × 17 = 289

Another nice thing about square numbers is that if you don't have pennies, and don't like to multiply either, you can find them by adding. Add up any string of odd numbers that are in order, starting with 1. For example, $1 + 3 + 5 = 9$, and you've already heard plenty about how square 9 is. Mathematicians say that any square number can be written as the sum of consecutive odd numbers.

Do you know how many squares there are on a checkerboard? There are 64 — a square number, of course. Prove it by one of these methods. Then see if you can find the largest square number that is less than 1,000. (Your calculator may help here.)

$$1 + 3 + 5 + 7$$
$$+ 9 + 11 + 13 =$$

49

Well, they *are* a little odd.

Strange Squares

Before you put away your calculator, look at this strange situation. Some pairs of square numbers have a peculiar characteristic. Take 144 and 441. They are the reverse of each other, right? To get 144, you can multiply 12 by 12; 441 is 21 times 21. And 12 and 21 are the reverse of each other as well!

This happens for 169 and 961 also.

$$13 \times 13 = 169$$
$$31 \times 31 = 961$$

It turns out that 12 and 13 are the only two-digit numbers that act this way. There are larger numbers that act like this, however.

$$112 \times 112 = 12,544$$
$$211 \times 211 = 44,521$$

Check this arithmetic with your calculator. Can you find any other squares that have this unusual trait?

144

441

Numbers Can Be Triangular Too

Numbers come in shapes other than squares. Some numbers are triangular. Get the pennies out again, and you can see why. You can arrange six pennies into a triangle, like this:

So 6 is considered to be a triangular number. Add another row and you have this:

Count them up. There are ten pennies, so 10 is a triangular number. Chop off two rows, and you have this:

That shows that 3 is a triangular number. Chop off one more row and you have only one penny; that's a triangular number also.

There's a pattern to these numbers. Look at them in order from smallest to largest: 1, 3, 6, 10. The next one is 15. Can you see a pattern in the way they grow?

I know about a **TWO-SHAPED NUMBER**. There is a triangular number smaller than 100 that is also square. Can you find it?

49

Take Your Time

Which is larger?

0+1+2+3+4+5

or

0×1×2×3×4×5

I hope I'll get to use my pennies for this.

You can't for one of them.

49

Pictures of Math

An Open Book

If you open this book so the two facing pages are numbered 40 and 41, the product of those two numbers is 1,640.

Just in case you've forgotten, the product is the answer to a multiplication problem.

Where do you need to open the book so that the product of the two facing page numbers is 12,656?

A Calendar Riddle

On New Year's Day, January 1, some relatives came to visit the family of a mathematical smarty pants. "How old are you?" the relatives asked.

SMACKO!

Smooch!

Smarty pants answered, "The day before yesterday I was 9 years old, and next year I will be 12 years old." This was true. Smarty pants's birthday is December 31. Can you explain this?

I thought you said she was smart.

Another Calendar Riddle

On what day will you celebrate having been alive for one billion seconds? How old will you be?

Can a person live that long?

I think we already have..

PART 3
Math for Two

I just learned a great game — it's called **Get to Zero**, and it's a counting game for two people.

Like a race to see who can count the fastest?

No, calm down, Speedo. You start at any number, say 25, then you take turns counting backwards. On your turn you can count 1, 2, or 3 numbers. So I could start by saying 25, 24, 23; or 25, 24; or just 25.

Then you start where I leave off. Whoever gets to zero wins.

Let's try it.

But there are five of us. Someone won't be able to play.

What are we going to do?

I'll play! I'll play! I can count! Listen: 25, 24, 23, 22, hee, hee, ha, ha, ha, hee, hee, hee, hee!

It's possible to figure out a way to win Get to Zero every time you play. That's the kind of thinking that makes games a part of the study of mathematics. In this chapter you'll have plenty of opportunity to learn games, and mathematical ways to analyze them. Find yourself a friend and give them a go.

Games Mathematicians Play

Games that interest mathematicians have one thing in common—they require strategy. Games that have mathematical interest aren't the helter-skelter games in which luck is the major force. They're games where there is a plan for action, games where decisions about which moves to make depend on some rule. That rule is the strategy.

What mathematicians search for in games is the "winning strategy." A winning strategy is a rule for playing so you'll win no matter what your opponent does. Playing a game like this isn't very interesting once you know the winning strategy. (That's what mathematicians say, although some kids might argue.) Figuring out the winning strategy is the fun part.

Sometimes it's not possible to come up with a winning strategy for a game, but it is possible to come up with a strategy that guarantees you won't lose. This is called a "drawing strategy." Tic-tac-toe is an example. When two crackerjack tic-tac-toe players get together, their games usually end in a draw, a tie. That's because there is no winning strategy for that game. The best you can do is to make sure you do not lose.

57

Race for New Year's Eve

This is a calendar game, but you don't need a calendar to play it. What you do need is a friend.

The idea of this game is to be the first one to say "December 31." There are several rules you must follow as you take turns saying dates. Whatever date you say must be later in the year than the date said before it, and you may change only the month *or* the day, not both.

Suppose the person who is first starts by saying "February 2." The next has to say a later date. It could be a later day in February, February 10, for example, a change only of the day. Or it could be a later month, keeping the same day, such as "March 2" or "June 2." You can skip months or days, but you can change only the month *or* day, and your date must be later in the year than the one said before it.

You might be wondering what in the world this has to do with mathematics. First of all, it's a game of strategy, and that's enough to make it a respectable addition to any mathematics book. Also, there's a winning strategy for this game. With some mental sleuthing, you can figure out whether it's a good idea to go first and what are good moves.

One way to work out a strategy is to think backwards. For instance, if you say January 31 (or the 31st of any month), your opponent can automatically win by leaving the 31 the same and changing the month to December. That's a legal move. Or if you say any day (except the 31st) in December, you're also sunk. As a matter of fact, if your opponent says November 30, you can't win. Can you figure out why? Starting with the end of the game and thinking backwards can give you some valuable clues.

What would happen if there were three of you playing? Is it possible to figure a winning strategy for a three-person game of Race for New Year's Eve?

Twists on Tic-Tac-Toe

Tic-tac-toe is a game with some advantages. It can be played nearly everywhere, and it can be played in any weather. The only equipment it takes is some paper and a pencil, and the rules are easy to learn.

It has a disadvantage also. It gets boring pretty fast, but don't give up on tic-tac-toe yet. With a few changes, you can play some variations on the game that will challenge the best of players.

Your Choice Tic-Tac-Toe. Take turns as you usually do. On your turn you may put down either an X or an O, and you can change your mind from turn to turn. So can your opponent. The winner is the one who finishes any row, column, or diagonal of all X's or all O's.

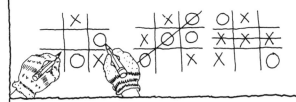

Number Tic-Tac-Toe. You don't use X's or O's for this version; you use the numbers from 1 to 9. Each number may be used only once in a game. Take turns writing a number in a space. The idea is to be the one to get the numbers in any row, column, or diagonal to add up to 15.

Last One Wins. The X's and O's don't matter so much in this game. The rule for play is this: On your turn, mark as many spaces as you like that are empty, as long as the ones you mark are all in the same row or column (not diagonal). Whoever fills in the last space is the winner.

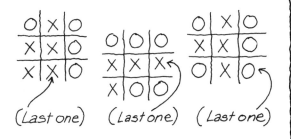

(Last one) (Last one) (Last one)

Tic-Tac-Toe for a Crowd. This game works well for from three to six people. You need a giant tic-tac-toe board to play on, one that is at least 10 by 10 instead of 3 by 3. Each of you chooses a different letter or mark or color crayon to use. The idea is the same as tic-tac-toe, except that instead of winning with three in a row, the winner has to get four in a row.

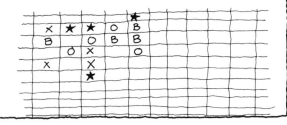

59

Keeping Track

Two kids were playing tic-tac-toe. The way they kept score was that at the end of each game the loser gave the winner a penny. When they stopped playing, one had won three games and the other had three more pennies than she started with. How many rounds had they played?

Having a Mathematical Conversation

You and a pal can see how sharp your mathematical conversation can be with this one. You need some objects to build with. They can be small blocks you have around the house— poker chips, dice, pencils, paper clips. It's essential that each of you has the same collection of stuff, exactly. Between six and ten objects will do.

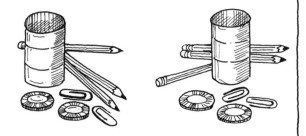

Now seat yourselves at a table and use a large box or cereal box to make a wall between you. The idea is that you can't see each other's working space.

One of you builds something with the objects. When you have built it, your job is to describe it well enough to the other person so that person can build exactly what you did. You can't see what your friend is building, and your friend can't see what you have built.

Your friend can ask questions, so it's a two-way conversation.

When you're both satisfied that you have done the best you can, lift the barrier and see how you did. Change roles and try again.

Which words helped and which did not? This game shows the need for good clear language and the ability to use that language well. How are you at mathematical talking?

Now, balance the third pencil on top of the can.

Bagels

Maybe you think bagels are something to eat. You're right. Maybe you also think that there has to be some reason, a really good one, for bagels to be included in a math book. Right again. And maybe you're thinking that including bagels in a math book probably has something to do with geometry, what with bagels being round and all. Well, you're wrong. In this math book, anyway, bagels have nothing to do with geometry, but everything to do with strategy.

"Bagels" is the name of a two-person game. It's a guessing game, but one that has a good deal of strategy to it. Each player thinks of a number; a three-digit number is good for starters. Take turns guessing each other's number. Whoever guesses the other person's number first wins.

Whenever one player makes a guess, the other gives some clues. Making good use of the clues is where the strategy comes in. There are three clues:

Pico means that one of the guessed digits is correct but is in the wrong place;
Fermi means that one of the guessed digits is correct and is also in the correct place;
Bagels (I'll bet you were wondering when the bagels part was coming in) means that none of the digits in the guess are correct.

If the guess contains more than one correct number, you give a combination clue such as **pico fermi** or **two fermi** or **two pico, one fermi**.

If Bagels whets your appetite for games, try it with four digits. Or more.

61

Guess My Word

Howdy! I'm **Weldon the Magic Bunny**, here to tell you about a two-person game that proves mathematics is everywhere, even in words. Here's how the game is played. One of the two of you thinks of a word — a three-letter word for starters. The other gets to guess it.

Box?

Nah.

Pie?

Nah.

Cap?

Nah.

Well, what is your word?

I keep telling you, it's "nah"!

Now that you've calmed down, we can continue with our rules. When one person makes a guess, the other has to tell whether the guess comes before or after the real word in the alphabet.

That way the game has some strategy to it, not just helter-skelter guessing. It's okay for the guesser to use paper and pencil to keep track of the guesses. Now try that one. And try to guess the other person's word in as few guesses as possible.

see?

The Thirty-one Game

This is a card game for two people. You don't need the entire deck to play. You need only 24 cards, ace through 6 of each of the four suits. If you don't have playing cards, you can make a set of 24 cards, with four of them numbered 1, four numbered 2, and so on up to four cards numbered 6. Lay out the 24 cards face up.

Decide who goes first. The first player turns any card face down and says that number out loud. The second player turns over any other card, adding that number to the first one. Continue taking turns turning a card face down and keeping a running total. Whoever reaches the sum of exactly 31 wins. If neither player hits 31, or if no one goes over 31, then no one wins that round.

There's a winning strategy to this game (you might have suspected as much). Which of you goes first is one important factor of the winning strategy, and which cards to turn over is the other.

If this game gets tiresome, change the total you're aiming for to 30, or 22, or 50. If you were to play for a total of 84, would you want to go first or second?

Race for Zero

Here is a calculator game for two people. You will need just one calculator. Whoever is first punches in a seven-digit number. The second player chooses one of the numerals showing and punches it in, repeating it as many times as he or she pleases, and subtracts it from what is already in the display. Then the first player takes the calculator again, chooses any numeral that is now showing, punches it in as many times as he or she likes, then subtracts it. Continue taking turns. The player who gets zero on the calculator display after subtracting wins the game.

PART 4
Logical Puzzles

You have to use logical reasoning to get the cards in order for Speedo's special deal. That means organizing your ideas and trying them out to see if they make sense. Skill in logical think-ing is necessary for understanding many mathematical concepts. You'll get lots of practice developing this skill from the problems in this chapter.

A Special Deal

It's easy to make the equipment for the special deal that Speedo showed Boots. Use playing cards, or number ten index cards or pieces of paper. It's not so easy, however, to arrange the cards so you can deal them out as Speedo did. If you can get someone else interested in solving this problem, life might be simpler. People have devised different ways for figuring out how to arrange the cards, and two different points of view may be useful.

Once you figure it out, you should be able to arrange the pile for any number of cards and have the system work. If you're using playing cards, try it with ace through king. And if you're still interested, here are two more versions to tackle.

1. Put two cards on the bottom each time instead of one.

2. Try it with a spelling twist. Start by spelling out the number ("one"). When you say "o," put a card on the bottom. When you say "n," put another card on the bottom, and do the same for "e." Turn over the fourth card, and it should be the 1. Now for 2. Put three cards on the bottom, one at a time, spelling "two," then turn over the next; it should be a 2. Continue all the way to the end.

Answer to *An Open Book*:
The pages are 112 and 113.

★$1 SENTENCE★

Prevent Inflation.

The Pizza Problems

This is the only known collection of mathematical pizza problems. You may have thought there was no mathematics in pizza. Well, there is. It turns out there is mathematics in plain cheese pizzas, sausage pizzas, pepperoni pizzas, pineapple pizzas, teriyaki pizzas, and avocado pizzas, just to name a few. (Sometimes, it's just not good to take mathematics too seriously.)

Pizza Problem No. 1. What time would it be if you gave one-eighth of a pizza to one friend and one-eighth of a pizza to another friend? Hint: Not only do you have to believe that mathematics can be silly at times, you have to add fractions to solve this one.

Pizza Problem No. 2. What looks exactly like half a pizza? Hint: This is another one that tests what you really know about fractions. The answer to this problem is not your neighbor's bulldog. You don't have to be told that wisecracks like that can hurt.

Pizza Problem No. 3. Why did Mr. Fibonacci ask to have his large cheese, pepperoni, salami, onion pizza cut into six pieces instead of eight? Hint: Some of the information in this problem is there just to throw you off the track. The most important clue isn't even in the problem, and it is that Mr. Fibonacci really doesn't understand much about fractions. When asked, he was unable to solve either of the first two problems.

Pizza Problem No. 4. How can you cut a pizza into eight slices, all the same shape and size, with only three cuts? Hint: You have to be willing to think messy for this one.

Pizza Problem No. 5. The favorite pizzas of Alicia, Mike, Patrick, and Sarah are anchovy, mushroom, pepperoni, and sausage. No one's name starts with the same letter as his or her favorite pizza. Mike and Sarah absolutely cannot stand anchovies, much less an anchovy pizza. Alicia and Mike know for sure that they hate pepperoni. What is each person's favorite pizza? Hint: To keep track of the information in a logical problem like this, it can help to make a chart for recording what you know.

	ANCHOVY	MUSHROOM	PEPPERONI	SAUSAGE
ALICIA				
MIKE				
PATRICK				
SARAH				

Pizza Problem No. 6. Jennifer and Steven's parents were planning to go on their yearly vacation to Coco Palms. Usually an adult comes to the house and stays with the kids. This year Jennifer and Steven begged and begged to be allowed to stay home alone, without any sitter. They promised to keep the house clean, do all their homework, and eat regularly.

Their parents said they'd agree, but on one condition. The condition was that Jennifer and Steven had to figure out how many days their parents would be gone. If they could, it would be proof that they were clever enough to deal with any problem that might come along.

It wasn't just a wild guess they had to make, however. Jennifer and Steven's mom was a mathematician, and she gave them a pizza problem to solve that would also give them the correct answer to their problem.

"Every night while we're away," their mom explained, "you'll have to eat at the local pizza parlor. And every night you have to order a different combination pizza, choosing two different ingredients from the list on the menu. How many nights will you have to eat there to have tried every possible combination pizza, each with two ingredients?"

Jennifer and Steven went down to the pizza parlor and got a menu. It listed 15 choices of ingredients.

How many different combination pizzas are there if each is made with 2 ingredients? Hint: If you'd like to think this problem through as a mathematician might, start small. Start with just 2 ingredients, and work your way up to 15. With 2 ingredients, pepperoni and sausage, for instance, there is only one possible pizza. If you add a third ingredient, meatball, then there are three possibilities: pepperoni-sausage, pepperoni-meatball, or sausage-meatball. Add a fourth and see what happens.

If you'd like to write like a mathematician as well as think like one, make a table. It can help you see the pizza pattern.

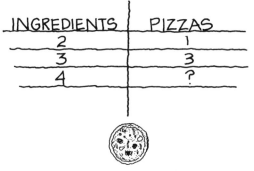

INGREDIENTS	PIZZAS
2	1
3	3
4	?

Pizza Problem No. 7. If it takes ten pizzamakers ten minutes to make ten pizzas, how long will it take five pizzamakers to make five pizzas?

Do you think they'll really be gone for three and a half months??

Good question. What's in Coco Palms, anyway?

September 4, 1974, was a great day in pizza history. At least it was in Little Rock, Arkansas. According to the Guinness Book of World Records, on that day the largest pizza was baked. It measured 25 feet 1 inch in diameter and weighed 1,200 pounds.

A Mathematical Tug-of-War

Your job in this mathematical contest is to decide who will win the final tug-of-war. The first two rounds give you the information you need.

The First Round. On one side there are four acrobats who have come down to the ground during the off-season for this special event. They have well-developed arm muscles because of all the swinging they do, and have proven themselves to be of equal strength. Remember that fact.

On the other side are five neighborhood grandmas, a tugging team that has practiced together for many, many years. They, too, are all equal in strength. Remember that fact also.

In the contest between these two teams, the result is dead even. Neither team can outtug the other. Remember that too.

The Second Round. One team is Ivan, the specially trained dog that got his start as a pup when he was taken out for a walk by his owner. Ivan gets pitted against a team made up of two of the grandmas and one acrobat.

Again, it's a draw—an equal pull. Remember that fact.

It's the final tug that you must figure out. It will be between these two teams: Ivan and three of the grandmas on one side, the four acrobats on the other. Can you figure out who will win this tug-of-war?

One way to solve this problem is to use algebra, a branch of mathematics that uses equations to deal with relationships between quantities. If you haven't learned about algebra yet, you'll have to rely on logical reasoning. Either way it's mathematical thinking you must do. Get a pencil and paper to help you tug on this problem.

★ THE FINAL ROUND ★

Ice Cream and the Three Little Pig Eyes

Every afternoon the three little pig eyes take an ice cream break. They head to the closest ice cream store, where each orders a double-dip cone. There are only two different kinds of double dips that the pig eyes ever order. It's either a double-dip vanilla cone or a licorice-chocolate combination. (If you think that's weird, you haven't heard anything yet. Keep reading.)

If pig eyes #1 orders vanilla-vanilla, then pig eyes #2 orders the other. Either pig eyes #1 or pig eyes #3 orders vanilla-vanilla, but they never do so on the same day. Pig eyes #2 and pig eyes #3 never both order the licorice-chocolate combination on the same day.

Which of the three little pig eyes ate a vanilla-vanilla cone yesterday and will order a licorice-chocolate cone today?

Would you like a **hint**? Two of the three pig eyes always order the same cone—every day! It may be easier to figure out who those are, then you'll know who's left to fill the answer slot.

Want another **hint**? A chart may help.

Are you wondering who in the world the little pig eyes are? See page 22.

	Yesterday	Today
#1		
#2		
#3		

Who's Who?

Rachel, Mark, Joshua, and Maria are 9, 10, 11, and 13 years old. Joshua is older than Maria and younger than Rachel. Mark is younger than Joshua and older than Maria. How old is each? Hint: A chart can help.

	9	10	11	13
RACHEL				
MARK				
JOSHUA				
MARIA				

Deal and Count

This is a solitaire card game that is easy to play, yet not so easy to understand mathematically. The easy part first: Shuffle a deck of cards. Then deal them out, one by one. While you're dealing, count: ace, 2, 3, 4, 5, 6, 7, 8, 9, 10, jack, queen, king, ace, 2, 3, 4, and so on. Each time you deal a card, turn it over so you can see what it is. You win this game of solitaire if you get to the end of a deck without turning over a card that matches what you count.

Get It?

There's no skill to this game, no strategy. However the cards get shuffled determines the results. It's pure chance. But pure chance is something that interests mathematicians very much. To study pure chance is to study the part of mathematics called "probability."

In this game your chance of winning, and getting to the end of the deck with no match, isn't too terrific—a little more than 1/3. That's less than a 50-50 chance of winning. Not very hopeful. It doesn't mean that you'll win one out of every three games. Mathematical probability doesn't make promises like that. A probability of 1/3 means that, if you play many, many games, the more you play, the closer your number of wins will be to exactly 1/3 of all the games you play.

Play Deal and Count a bunch of times and keep track of your number of wins and number of games. Don't get frustrated when you lose—you're a mathematician, remember?

King Arthur's Problem

King Arthur had a problem. His daughter, Glissanda, loved mathematics so much that she spent most of her time solving problems, making geometric designs, and playing with numbers. That wasn't King Arthur's problem; he was proud of his daughter and her mathematical interest. Glissanda had reached the age when a young woman was permitted to marry, and she was definitely interested in marrying. In fact, she had one requirement for a husband: he must love mathematics (or at least like it a lot). For her, a life of evenings in front of a warm fire solving mathematical puzzles seemed like a sure way to marital bliss. Finding that mathematics-loving husband was King Arthur's problem.

Now, if this story had taken place in modern times, King Arthur wouldn't have had this problem. Glissanda would probably have met someone in her math classes who would be a fine mate, and that would be that. But in the days of King Arthur and his Knights of the Round Table, women didn't have much freedom; their husbands were chosen by their parents.

Now King Arthur loved Glissanda dearly, and he would do anything for his daughter, but he was confused about how to find a husband to suit Glissanda. After all, the Knights of the Round Table—they were the best men in the land—were outdoor types who spent their time bravely scouting the countryside for dragons to slay. He couldn't remember any of them ever even mentioning mathematics.

King Arthur was perplexed. He thought about it for days. And days stretched into weeks, but no ideas came to him.

Meanwhile he had his kingly work to do, but he became so distracted by this marriage problem that he couldn't concentrate. King Arthur was definitely not himself. One morning at the meeting he was very short-tempered with his knights. Little things seemed to bother him. At one point he even shouted out, "Can't you control that constant clanking of your armor and sit still?" The knights knew he must have something important on his mind.

That night at dinner King Arthur talked to Glissanda about the situation. "How shall I find out who is the cleverest in mathematics?" he asked her. "Should I just ask?"

"No, no," protested Glissanda. "That wouldn't be a good way. Some would answer yes just to become next in line to be king. I could get stuck with a husband who wants to do nothing at night except drink ale, one with no true interest in mathematical conversation. You must devise a mathematical test."

"What sort of test?" King Arthur asked.

"Let me think about it," Glissanda answered, wandering off, already deep in thought.

The next morning at breakfast Glissanda seemed cheerful.

"Do you have the test?" her father asked.

"Not yet," Glissanda answered, "but I'm working on it. Tell me, father, how many knights are there at your Round Table?"

"Well, that varies," he replied. "It depends on how many are back from a journey. Sometimes as many as 50, and sometimes only a handful. Why?"

But Glissanda didn't answer. King Arthur could tell she was lost in thought, with that glaze over her eyes that told him she was thinking about mathematics again. It made him think that her husband would need to be very understanding.

That night at dinner Glissanda made an announcement. "I've got the test," she said. "You can give it at your meeting tomorrow to the Knights of the Round Table."

King Arthur's face broke into a relieved smile. "Wonderful, wonderful!" he exclaimed. "But what if all the knights aren't present tomorrow? You know, I never can tell who will come."

"I've thought of that," Glissanda said. "In this test there is just one problem. Give it tomorrow to the knights who are present and announce that those interested in answering should reappear in one month's time with their solutions. In the meanwhile, they should spread the problem throughout the kingdom, so others who are off doing what knights do can come with solutions as well."

"What is the problem?" King Arthur asked eagerly.

Glissanda explained, "Suppose 24 knights came to a meeting of the Round Table. And suppose the 24 chairs were numbered in order, so that everyone knew which chair was number 1, and in which direction you will count to 24. In order to choose my husband, you draw your sword, point to the knight in the first chair, and say, 'You live.' Then point to the knight in chair number 2, say, 'You die,' and chop off his head. To the third knight you say, 'You live.' And to the fourth, you say, 'You die,' and chop off his head. You continue doing this around and around the circle, chopping off the head of every other living knight until just one is left. That's the one I'll marry.

Glissanda stopped talking.

"That's it?" her father asked, horrified. "You expect me to kill all of my knights but one? What kind of kingdom would I have then? There would be just you, your husband, a roomful of dead knights, and the rest of my knights cowering in the countryside for fear of ever returning to the Round Table. Is this what you call mathematics? Have you gone crazy?" King Arthur was shouting now. He couldn't believe his ears. He wanted Glissanda to be happy, but this was ridiculous.

"Oh, father," Glissanda said. "I wouldn't expect you to actually kill anyone. It's just a problem, and it definitely is mathematical. Besides," she went on, giggling a bit, "if you don't tell them you really won't chop heads, then only the brave knights will come. Then I'm sure to have a husband with courage as well as one with mathematical intelligence."

"But Glissanda," King Arthur went on, still rather upset, "I admit it's an unusual problem that is a true test of logical thought. But how do you know 24 knights will return that day to find the solution?"

Glissanda giggled a bit more, feeling even merrier. "That's the real point to the problem," she said. "Don't tell, but the knight of my dreams would know that he has solved the problem only if he knows where to sit for *any* number of chairs. I've been working on this problem, and there's a marvelous pattern for the solution!"

Which seat is the right one when there are 24 knights at the Round Table? Can you find the pattern for predicting which is the right seat for any number of chairs?

Logical Breakfast

The three little pig eyes have different ideas about what to eat for breakfast. Actually they have different ideas about almost everything, but this story is about breakfast. One of the pig eyes loves to eat granola with orange juice poured over it. Another of the little tricksters likes scrambled eggs with ketchup. The other likes to have a banana split, claiming that it helps one keep a sharp eye out for the unusual in life.

Your job, and it's a mathematical one, of course, is to find out which of the little pig eyes eats the banana splits for breakfast. To find out, you have to use some logical reasoning; it's difficult to tell just by looking at them.

(GARURP!)

Some **clues** about the lineup.
★ Pig eyes #1 does not eat scrambled eggs with ketchup or banana splits.
★ Pig eyes #2 does not eat scrambled eggs with ketchup. Those are all the clues you get. The rest is up to you.

Answer to *Take Your Time*:

Adding the numbers from 0 to 5 will be larger since 0 times anything is always 0.

80

What's a Paradox?

Every once in a while mathematics runs into a kind of snag called a "paradox." This happens when something seems to make sense, and at the same time it seems impossible for it to make sense. A paradox is a contradiction and can make the best of mathematicians sit up and take notice.

There are different kinds of paradoxes. One is where something seems rather incredible, but because it can be proved to you, you have to accept it, even if it drives your imagination nuts. Optical illusions can be like that. Which of the two pencils is longer? Measure them to find out for sure.

An Infinite Paradox. In another kind of paradox, a contradiction appears because you've reasoned incorrectly about something. Most people think that a whole thing is always greater than any of its parts. That's true for an apple or a chocolate cake or anything you can hold and touch. But it's not always so in mathematics. Ideas can't always be held or touched and have to be examined in your mind.

Here's an example. Take all the counting numbers—1, 2, 3, 4, and so on. There are more of them than anyone can count, because no matter how far you go, you can always count one more. And then one more. And then one more, and so on. That's why mathematicians say that the set of counting numbers is infinite.

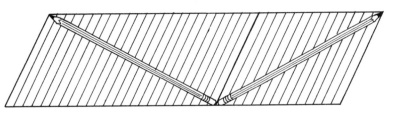

Now think about part of that set of counting numbers, just the odd numbers—1, 3, 5, 7, and so on. Since you skip every other one, you may think that there are half as many odd numbers as there are counting numbers. That may seem like a reasonable way to think, but it's wrong. That set of odd numbers is also infinite. It goes on and on forever.

You can't say that one infinite set is larger than another infinite set, since neither set will ever run out. (Weird things happen in the world of the infinite!) Incorrect reasoning can lead you to say something is true when it isn't, and there you are in the middle of a paradox.

The Line Paradox. There are many examples of paradoxes from incorrect reasoning in geometry. The line paradox is one that is centuries old. Trace the figure below onto a piece of paper so you can cut it out.

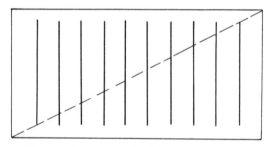

Count the lines inside the rectangle to make sure you believe there are ten of them. Now cut the rectangle along the dotted line, and slide the lower piece down and to the left, to the position shown below.

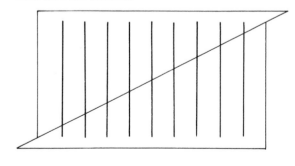

Count the lines inside the figure now. There are only nine! How did a line vanish? If you slide the lower part back, the missing line reappears. But where did it come from?

What happens is that no single line vanishes. Because of the way the rectangle is cut, 8 of the original 10 lines were cut into 2 pieces. Then there were 18 pieces of lines (count them in the original drawing to be sure you understand this), which got rearranged into 9 lines. Each of those 9 lines is longer than each of the original 10 lines were. There's still as much total line; it has just gotten redistributed. To think that a line vanished is incorrect reasoning and will never help you figure out a paradox.

The same idea has been used to make this puzzle. Trace these faces onto a piece of paper, cut on the dotted line, and slide the lower piece to the left. It will seem as if a face has disappeared! Can you explain this?

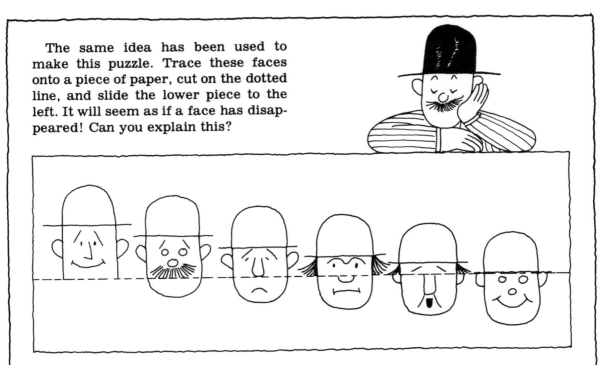

The Checkerboard Paradox. This is another geometric paradox, but this time an extra square seems to appear, rather than vanish. You start with an 8 by 8 square, ruled off into 64 squares, just like a checkerboard. Draw the lines inside as shown, label the pieces, then cut carefully on the lines drawn.

Rearrange the four pieces into a rectangle as shown.

Now you have a rectangle with 65 squares! See if you can figure out how to explain this paradox.

There is still another type of paradox—the logical paradox. This type can get quite complicated. Some of them have caused such confusion among mathematicians that, for some, explanations have not yet been found. Following are two for you to unravel.

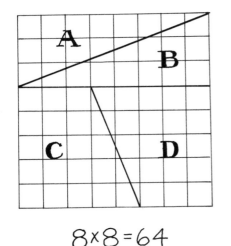

$8 \times 8 = 64$

$5 \times 13 = 65$

The Barber Paradox. The only barber in a small village had a sign in his window.

This barber shaves everyone in the village who does not shave himself. No exceptions.

The sign caught the eye of a mathematician passing by. Actually it was the "No exceptions" that she noticed. This mathematician believed that every rule probably has exceptions.

What she wondered about was this: Did the barber shave himself? And that's when the paradox appeared. If the barber shaved himself, then he was shaving someone who did shave himself—himself—and that was breaking his own rule. But if he didn't shave himself, then, according to his own sign, he had to come to him to be shaved, since he shaved everyone who did not shave himself. No exceptions. Either way, he contradicts his own sign.

The mathematician pointed out this paradox to the barber. As the legend has it, he was never quite the same again.

One Last Paradox. If you can stand it, give this last one a try. Read it carefully first.

> 1. *This book has 300 pages.*
> 2. *The author of this book is Regina Carter.*
> 3. *The statements numbered 1, 2, and 3 are all false.*

For sure number 1 is false. (You can count for yourself if you don't believe the page numbers.) And for sure number 2 is false. Regina Carter has always hated mathematics, and probably always will, and would never be caught fooling around with math books (or paradoxes). But what about number 3? If it's true that statement 3 is false, then shouldn't 1 and 2 really be true, and how can something be both true and false at the same time? That's a paradox, which may be the only thing you're sure of now.

Want to know what I think about paradoxes? It would be a great name for a rock group — **The Paradoxes**. It fits perfectly. A rock group is supposed to play music, right? Well, for *my* ear, what they play is noise, garbage, not music. There's a contradiction for you. Yep, **The Paradoxes** would make it big, I bet.

Paradoxes in mathematics are not useless and silly tricks. They may be worth a laugh, or at least one hah, but that's not where their true worth lies. Paradoxes make you think about ideas and make you question what seems—but maybe it isn't—right. That kind of thinking is useful for many things, not only mathematics.

The Möbius strip I'm standing on on page 81 is a paradox. Paper has two sides, right? How many sides does a Möbius strip have?

Some people think that the strangest paradox of all is that there can be paradoxes in mathematics. They think that mathematics ought to be above that sort of perplexing thinking. It's not so, though. The Greeks first explored paradoxes, and even today new ones are being discovered. If you're interested in them, you may have a mathematical career cut out for you.

Is there a paradox lurking in this $1 sentence?

★ $1 SENTENCE ★

Surely highways prevent problems.

What's Odd About This?

If you try this problem at the dinner table, you might get your parents so interested that they will forget you haven't eaten your broccoli. But then again, you might not. In either case there's some mathematics here worth trying.

For this problem you need three cups and 11 objects. Coins or paper clips will work—any objects that will fit inside the cups. Here's the problem. Put the 11 objects into the three cups so that there are an odd number of objects in each cup. How many ways can you do it so that each arrangement is different?

That problem shouldn't give you much trouble. But before you put away the cups and objects and get back to your broccoli, try this one. Get rid of one of the objects, so you have three cups and ten objects. Now try the same problem, still trying to put an odd number of objects in each cup. This time, it's not so obvious. It can be done, but there's a trick to it. Using the trick, one person claims there are 10 different ways. Another claim is 15 different ways, using another trick.

Since a trick is needed here, and that doesn't seem quite mathematically fair, here's a hint: Can you find a way for an object to be in two cups at the same time?

In case the hint doesn't help and you're going nuts, there is one solution to this problem in the book. Finding it is up to you, though. (We can't tell everything!)

Statistics are important for lots of people — toy manufacturers, for example, who need to learn what kinds of toys and games will appeal to kids; policemen who need to know about traffic patterns in order to decide where new lights or stop signs are needed; television producers who need to know what kinds of television shows will have appeal; newscasters who want to know about the popularity of candidates during elections; shoe-store owners who need to know how many of each shoe size to stock; and on and on. Collecting and analyzing statistics is an important part of mathematics. Here's your chance to learn about statistics, and even to collect some yourself.

Beat it! Pig eyes aren't in this survey!

The Mathematics of a Pencil

Every year Americans buy approximately 2½ billion pencils, the regular kind that is usually yellow and needs sharpening from time to time. That's a lot of pencils—an average of one each month for every person.

The kind of pencil you use today, with a round lead inside, was invented over 100 years ago, in 1879. Before then the lead in pencils was square and not so easy to use. Actually it's not correct to say the lead is either round or square since it really isn't "lead" at all. It's a mixture of graphite and clay; lead never was used in pencils. But graphite used to be called "black lead," so that's probably why we still refer to it as lead.

Getting all the ingredients for making a batch of pencils is a task of worldwide proportions. The wood comes from cedar trees on the Pacific Coast of the United States. Clay comes from the state of Georgia. Graphite comes from Madagascar. Also used are wax from the carnauba palm tree of Brazil and a gum called "tragacanth" from the Middle East.

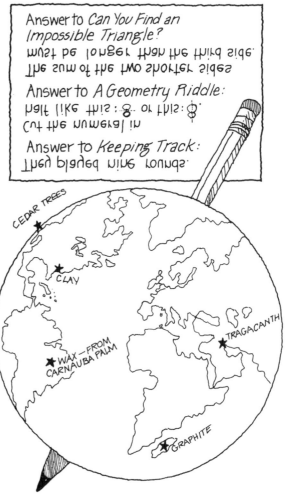

Answer to *Can You Find an Impossible Triangle?*
The sum of the two shorter sides must be longer than the third side.

Answer to *A Geometry Riddle:*
Cut the numeral in half like this: 8 or this: ∅

Answer to *Keeping Track:*
Then played nine rounds.

Perhaps this doesn't sound like stuff for a book on mathematics. It seems to belong in a history book or a geography book. So let's get to the mathematics part—statistics. Pencil statistics.

If you laid a year's supply of pencils end to end, they would circle the earth 5 times.

One pencil can be sharpened approximately 17 times.

One pencil can be used to write about 45,000 words.

Now, Suzanne, write "I will not throw pencils in class" until you have used up that brand new pencil.

One pencil can draw a line about 33½ miles long (56 kilometers, if you're thinking metric).

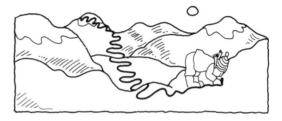

That means a year's supply could trace the distance to the moon and back about 200,000 times.

You should be able to make about 4,000 checkmarks with a pencil before you absolutely must sharpen it.

America's 100 billionth pencil was manufactured in 1976 and was displayed at the Smithsonian Institute.

Had enough? If not, see if you can find out what it means when a pencil is a number 2, or 2½, or 1, or 3. Now warm up your calculator. If the same number of pencils continued to be made each year (2½ billion), in what year will the quintillionth be made? Or the nonillionth? Or the tredecillionth? (Check page 121 if you have no idea what these words of enormity mean.)

★$1 SENTENCE★

Writing upsets Suzanne.

Food Statistics

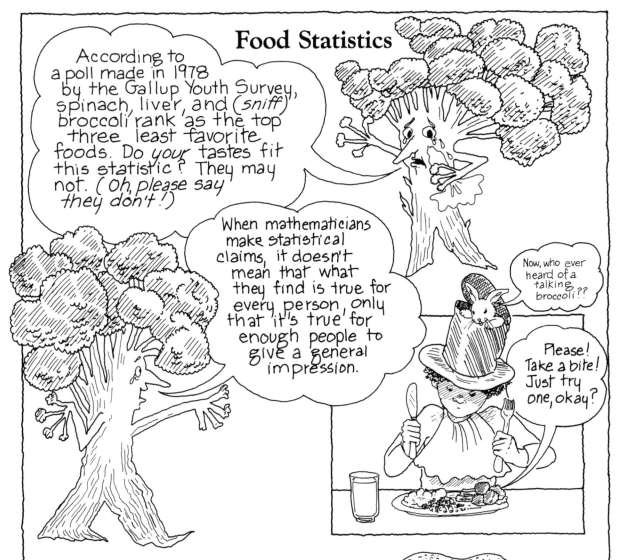

According to a poll made in 1978 by the Gallup Youth Survey, spinach, liver, and *(sniff)* broccoli rank as the top three least favorite foods. Do *your* tastes fit this statistic? They may not. *(Oh, please say they don't!)*

When mathematicians make statistical claims, it doesn't mean that what they find is true for every person, only that it's true for enough people to give a general impression.

Now, who ever heard of a talking broccoli??

Please! Take a bite! Just try one, okay?

You have to look at statistics with a sharp eye. They can be misleading. Though the poll revealed that spinach was the least favorite food of kids, it was 20 percent of the kids asked who reported that their least favorite food was spinach. That's only one out of every five kids asked! It's true that spinach led the list of least favorites, but it wasn't even the opinion of half the kids asked. With liver, 19 percent of the kids polled gave it as their least favorite. And 8 percent named broccoli. Other kids gave different choices: vegetables in general, beans, peas, and fish.

When kids were asked about their favorite foods, the top four winners were Italian food, steak, hamburgers, and chicken or turkey. Other favorites listed included seafood, vegetables, potatoes, Mexican food, and fish. (Notice that vegetables and fish made both the favorite and the least favorite categories. There is no pleasing everyone when it comes to taste.)

Be a Pollster

How about taking your own survey and seeing how the results you get compare with the results of the Gallup survey? There are several different ways you can do it. See which makes the most sense to you.

Food Poll Number 1. Prepare two lists of foods that correspond to the foods reported on the Gallup survey. The two lists shown below list foods in the order that the poll produced. You might want to mix up the order, and then, after your results are in, see if your final ranking is the same as that of the Gallup results. You'll need another copy of each list on which to tally the response you get.

Food Poll Number 2. Don't have lists for kids to choose from. Just ask two questions: What is your favorite food? What is your least favorite food? Then compare your results with those of the Gallup survey.

There are other things you might also be interested in finding out. For example, do girls and boys have different tastes? The Gallup survey showed that girls and boys have tastes which are pretty much the same, but girls seem to dislike liver and spinach more than boys do, and like Italian food a little better. What about adults' tastes? Are they the same as kids' tastes, or are they different? Make a prediction, then poll some adults and compare.

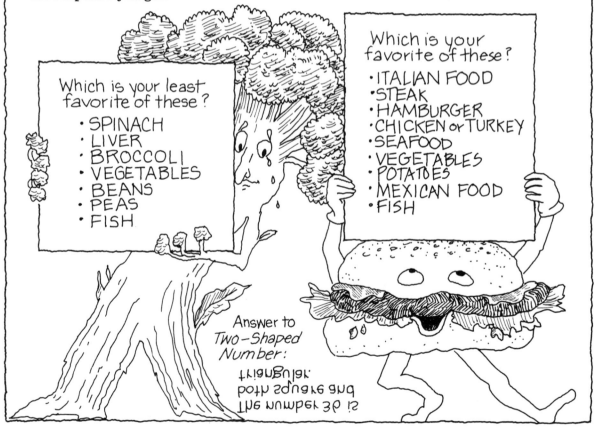

Which is your least favorite of these?
- SPINACH
- LIVER
- BROCCOLI
- VEGETABLES
- BEANS
- PEAS
- FISH

Which is your favorite of these?
- ITALIAN FOOD
- STEAK
- HAMBURGER
- CHICKEN or TURKEY
- SEAFOOD
- VEGETABLES
- POTATOES
- MEXICAN FOOD
- FISH

Answer to Two-Shaped Number:
The number 36 is both square and triangular.

The Mathematics of Polls

Taking polls that produce valid results deals with the branch of mathematics called "statistics." There really is no way to find out absolutely what is the least or most favorite food of kids; you can't possibly ask every kid in the world. The results of surveys and polls are based on asking just a part of the entire population, a "sample," it's called. How large a sample is an important factor when reporting reliable and believable results. The size of a sample may depend on the purpose of the poll.

Suppose you're polling kids' food preferences. How many kids you ask is important. If you're planning to invite six friends for a party, you may be able to ask all of them what they like to eat. That would be a poll of the entire population of party guests and would certainly be a sound statistical survey for your purpose. Planning your menu around what only one kid said is not as sensible. Polling five may do fine. But if you polled those six kids, then used that information to give a general report about which foods kids in the United States like and dislike, your results wouldn't be worth much statistically. So sample size is important.

Another consideration is where you get your sample. If you found that half or more of the kids you surveyed named Mexican food as their favorite, it may be true only where you live. There are some parts of the country where tacos and other Mexican food aren't popular, or even available. Some kids may love grits or pot stickers; others may never have tasted them. The makeup of your sample is an important factor in what results you report.

As you study more mathematics, you'll have the chance to learn more about statistics and how they're used. Getting some experience now can come in handy later.

The Exclamation Explanation

In mathematics, 3! is a special number. It's not excited. That's not what the exclamation point is about. The exclamation point tells you that 3! is equal to 6. Well, that's what it tells mathematicians. Confused? You deserve an explanation. There's no room for confusion in mathematical thought. Things are tough enough without confusion.

The language first. How do you say "3!" out loud? You don't shout it. You say "three factorial." In mathematics the "!" stands for "factorial." That doesn't tell you much, but at least it's a start. Someone came along with a name for this funny creature, 3!, before you or I did, and we all go along with it.

The meaning second. Suppose you and two friends go into an ice cream store for cones. "Who's first?" the person behind the counter might ask. And when the first kid has received a cone, the person would most likely ask, "Who's next?" Well, how many different possibilities are there for you and your friends to be first, second, and third? The answer to that is 6—see if you can prove that to yourself before going on any farther. Then come back and continue reading.

Ready? The reason that 3! is equal to 6 is that if there are three of you in line for ice cream cones, then there are six different ways you could line up.

Oh no.

Suppose 4 of you went for ice cream cones. How many different ways could the 4 of you line up? Can you work that out so you get 24? It's true that 4! equals 24.

Whew!

I could sure use some ice cream!

Figuring out how many ways there are to line up if there are five of you is an even bigger task. It can be done, and you might like to try it. But mathematicians are the kind of people who would rather look for the easy way to do something, even if it takes twice as long.

It's no use working out all the ways for five people to line up,

a mathematician might say,

because then I'll be stuck working out how many ways six can line up, and then seven, and so on. If I figure out a way to work the five-in-a-line problem, I'll have a method to use for any number.

Time to back up and think like a mathematician. With one person, there is only one way to line up, so 1! equals 1. With two people, there are two ways to line up, so 2! equals 2. Here's all the information so far.

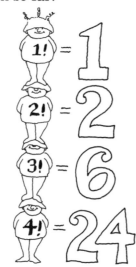

$1! = 1$

$2! = 2$

$3! = 6$

$4! = 24$

And it turns out that, as in all of mathematics, there's a pattern for getting each of these with some simple arithmetic.

$$1! = 1 = 1$$
$$2! = 2 = 1 \times 2$$
$$3! = 6 = 1 \times 2 \times 3$$
$$4! = 24 = 1 \times 2 \times 3 \times 4$$

According to this pattern, to figure 5!, multiply $1 \times 2 \times 3 \times 4 \times 5$, which is 120. Try 6! this way to see if you get 720.

Back to the ice cream line. It's not that ice cream has anything to do with factorial numbers. It was just an example to help you figure out how many ways there are to line up something. It's just the kind of problem that some mathematicians love. The exclamation idea is just an abbreviation. It's quicker to write 10!, for example, than to write $1 \times 2 \times 3 \times 4 \times 5 \times 6 \times 7 \times 8 \times 9 \times 10$; it also takes up less room than the value of 10!, which is 3,628,800. Factorial numbers get very big very fast, so the shorthand symbol comes in handy.

Here are factorials up to 15.

0!	1
1!	1
2!	2
3!	6
4!	24
5!	120
6!	720
7!	5,040
8!	40,320
9!	362,880
10!	3,628,800
11!	39,916,800
12!	479,001,600
13!	6,227,020,800
14!	87,178,291,200
15!	1,307,674,368,000

If everyone in your class at school lined up every day before going home, and there were 30 students, and you came to school every single day of the year, not even skipping weekends or holidays, it would take you almost 7 nonillion years before you had lined up every possible way. (Check page 121 for what nonillion means.) For sure, 30! is an enormous number!

One last note, for only the mathematically brave at heart. How come, on the chart above, 0! is equal to 1? Having zero people line up for ice cream cones is a ridiculous idea, and doesn't help much mathematically. But mathematicians hate to leave any idea unexplored. They do rely on patterns to help them explore ideas, and here's the pattern that has convinced mathematicians that 0! is definitely equal to 1. See if you are convinced by it. Get out your calculator.

$$6! \div 5! = 6$$
$$5! \div 4! = 5$$
$$4! \div 3! = 4$$
$$3! \div 2! = 3$$
$$2! \div 1! = 2$$

To continue this pattern, $1! \div 0! = 1$. If not, the pattern breaks down, which makes mathematicians very sad. Even nervous. That's just how mathematics works: patterns are not supposed to break down.

So 0! has to be equal to 1, because 1 divided by 1 is the only way to get 1. Can you follow this? If not, don't worry.

It may make sense to you some day. But even if it doesn't, you can still get in line for ice cream cones, whether or not you understand any factorials.

One *more* last note. If you have 15 books on a shelf and are thinking about rearranging them into all the possible lineups, you had better think twice. Even if you could rearrange them once every minute, it would take you over 2 million years to try all the possible lineups.

Lining Up

If everyone living in the 48 continental United States lined up around the border of the country, holding hands with arms outstretched, would we have enough people to go around? Would there be extras?

Some facts might help here. The border is about 12,400 miles. The average height of a person in our country is about 64 inches. And since people usually can stretch their arms to about the same distance as their height, each person would use up 64 inches of the border. And one more fact. There are about 220 million people living in the 48 states.

Heart Beating

The average person's heart beats 103,680 times a day. How many heartbeats is this in 1 minute? To find your own heartbeat rate, take your pulse for 15 seconds; multiply that by 4 to find the number of heartbeats per minute. If you don't know how to take your pulse, ask an adult to help you.

Answer to A Mathematical Tug-of-War:

Grandmothers will win. Ivan and the three

Probability

Write the numbers from 1 to 4 on a piece of paper, like this:

1 2 3 4

Then ask someone to circle one of the numbers. From a statistical study where this experiment was done many, many times, a mathematical theory of probability resulted: four out of five people will circle the number 3. Do you think this would be true if *you* carried out the experiment? Try it and find out.

In case your experimental subjects want to know what you're doing, tell them this:

I'm doing a statistical experiment to test a theory of probability.

Whoo-pee-doo.

This answer may satisfy some, but others might want additional information. Here's some more of the mathematical scoop about this kind of experiment.

Collecting statistics is a way to get a picture of a particular situation, a kind of numerical picture. It can be useful for predicting what is likely to happen in a situation where you don't have all the statistics. If you ask people to circle one of the numbers in the 1—2—3—4 experiment, chances are pretty good that most of them will circle the number 3; the probability is four out of five, or 4/5 as mathematicians would write it.

The "four-out-of-five" information doesn't promise that if you try the experiment on five people, four of them will circle the 3 and the other will circle one of the other numbers. Probability doesn't work like that. Probability theory *does* promise that if you do this experiment many times, the more times you try the experiment, the closer the results will come to the 4/5 probability. That's what the odds favor.

So far the leader is **2**.

Answer to *Logical Breakfast:* big ones #2 eats banana split for breakfast.

99

Cross-Country Traveling

All the following people have crossed the United States and have been written about in the *Guinness Book of World Records*. Can you match the person to the number of days?

1. In 1973 Paul Cornish peddled from San Francisco to New York City in ? days.

2. Clinton Shaw skated from New York to Santa Monica, California, in 1974. This skate took him ? days.

3. John Lees walked from Los Angeles to New York City in 1972. It took him ? days.

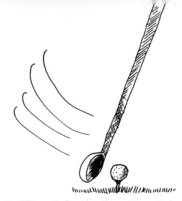

5. Floyd Satterlee Rood took 114,737 strokes to hit golf balls across the United States from the Pacific to the Atlantic. It took him ? days, and he lost 3,511 balls on the trip.

6. David Ryder went from Los Angeles to New York City on crutches. He did this in 1970 in ? days.

4. Charles Creighton and James Hargis drove their car in reverse from New York City to Los Angeles. The car they drove was a Ford Model A 1929 roadster, and they made the trip in 1930. It took them ? days.

a. 13.22 days
b. 18 days
c. 53.51 days
d. 77 days
e. 137 days
f. 384 days

PART 6
Math Trickery

What Billy does is to take the string and make a knot so the halfway mark is in the loop. Then when he cuts, the cup won't drop! What does this have to do with mathematics? It's a logical solution to a tricky problem. Some people think there's no place in mathematics for trickery. Well, that's just not so, and this chapter of mathemagic aims to show you why. Try these tricks for yourself if you need convincing, or even if you don't.

The Incredible Memory Whiz

Here's a chance for a spectacular magic trick to be performed by an incredible memory whiz: you. Copy this chart on a piece of paper.

There's Billy's phone number!

(31) 2460662	(27) 8314594	(35) 6404482	(48) 9549325	(20) 1347189	(42) 3583145	(36) 7415617
(2) 3145943	(45) 6516730	(30) 1459437	(34) 5493257	(25) 6392134	(6) 7189763	(15) 6280886
(23) 4370774	(39) 0550550	(18) 9213471	(22) 3369549	(4) 5167303	(38) 9437077	(16) 7291011
(21) 2358314	(5) 6178538	(44) 5505505	(11) 2246066	(41) 2572910	(19) 0336954	(8) 9101123
(49) 0662808	(14) 5279651	(24) 5381909	(47) 8538190	(26) 7303369	(40) 1561785	(28) 9325729
(9) 0224606	(37) 8426842	(46) 7527965	(3) 4156178	(1) 2134718	(17) 8202246	(32) 3471897
(29) 0448202	(12) 3257291	(33) 4482022	(13) 4268426	(43) 4594370	(7) 8190998	(10) 1235831

Give the chart to someone. Ask that person to tell you a number in any circle, and say that you'll write the seven digits that are written below that number. That person will think you've got a pretty astounding memory—wrong. All you have to do is to use a bit of mathemagics and follow this pattern. Whatever number you're given, do this:

1. Add 11 to the number.

2. Reverse the answer you get, and write down those two numbers.

3. Add them. If the sum is less than 10, write it down. If it's greater than 10, just write down what's in the ones place.

4. Keep doing this, adding the last two numbers you get, writing down just what is in the ones place of that sum, until you get all seven digits.

Here's a sample: Suppose someone picks 49.

1. Add 11. That gives you 60.

2. Reverse the digits and write down 06, the first two of the seven digits.

3. Add 0 and 6. This gives 6. Write it down.

4. Add the 6 and 6. This gives 12. Keep only the number in the ones place, the 2. Now you have four of the digits: 0662.

5. Add 6 and 2, and write down the 8: 06628.

6. Add 2 and 8, and write just the 0. You have six of them now: 066280.

7. The last one is 8 plus 0, another 8: 0662808.

To really dazzle someone with your powers of memory, make up your own chart following this procedure, putting 12 or more digits under each circle.

Isn't That Sum-thing?

Here's one of the most dazzling answer-before-the-problem tricks. It's a truly wondrous act of addition. Ask someone in the audience for a three-digit number. Write it for all to see. Leave spaces for four more numbers and draw a line. Suppose the number you were given is 645; here's what you write.

645

On a slip of paper, after a moment of mathematical concentration, write a number and give it to someone to hold until the end of the trick. You get the number you write down by putting a 2 in front of the number you were given (2,645) and then subtracting 2 from it (2,645 - 2 = 2,643). So it's 2,643 that the person gets to hold.

You then ask for a second three-digit number; write it under the first one. Suppose you're given 473.

You write down a third number: 526.

Ask for a fourth number from the audience. Suppose it's 128.

Then you write the fifth: 871.

Now, with a little help from the audience, add up the five numbers. The answer will match the number you wrote on that slip of paper. Isn't that sum-thing?

The trick is in the two numbers you write. When you're given the second number, subtract each digit from 9 to write the third. Do the same with the fourth to get the fifth. This way the sum of each of the last two pairs of numbers adds up to 999. So you're really adding 999 twice, for a total of 1,998, to whatever number you were given to start with. That you know ahead of time. Well, 1,998 is 2,000 minus 2. That's why you have to add the 2 in front (in the thousands place) and subtract 2 from the original number. (What would the answer be if you have the audience pick a sixth number, and you pick a seventh before the final addition?)

The Calendar Caper

You'll need a month from an old calendar for this trick. Have someone draw around a square block of numbers, four by four.

When that has been done, you write a number on a slip of paper and hand it to someone to hold. Then you turn your back and give these instructions:

1. Circle any one date in the blocked-off square.
2. Cross out all the other numbers in the row and column that the circled number is in.
3. Now circle another number.
4. Again cross out the other numbers in the row and column the second number is in.
5. Do this again for a third number.
6. There should be only one date left that isn't circled or crossed out. Circle it.
7. Add up the circled dates.

Then you ask the person holding the slip of paper to read the number on it. It's the same as the total of the circled numbers!

To get the correct number to write on the slip of paper, you add the dates of two opposite corners and double the sum. This magic will work for any square block this size on any month.

Sun	Mon	Tues	Wed	Thurs	Fri	Sat
		1	2	3	4	5
6	7	8	9	10	11	12
13	14	15	16	(17)	18	19
20	21	22	23	24	25	26
27	28	29	30			

Sun	Mon	Tues	Wed	Thurs	Fri	Sat
		1	2	3	4	5
6	7	8	9	10	11	12
13	14	15	16	(17)	18	19
20	21	22	23	24	(25)	26
27	28	29	30			

Sun	Mon	Tues	Wed	Thurs	Fri	Sat
		1	2	3	4	5
6	7	8	9	10	11	(12)
13	14	15	16	(17)	18	19
20	21	22	23	24	(25)	26
27	28	29	30			

Sun	Mon	Tues	Wed	Thurs	Fri	Sat
		1	(2)	3	4	5
6	7	8	9	10	11	(12)
13	14	15	16	(17)	18	19
20	21	22	23	24	(25)	26
27	28	29	30			

Calculator Tricks

Announce that you are very fortunate because the calculator you have not only adds, subtracts, multiplies, and divides, but it helps you do magic as well. Then proceed to use it to help you do these tricks.

The Favorite-Number Trick. Give someone the magic calculator and have him (suppose it's a boy) punch in this number: thirty-seven thousand thirty-seven. Then check to see that the calculator reads 37,037. Ask him for his favorite number between 1 and 9. Whatever number he gives you, multiply it by 3 in your head, and tell him to multiply what he has already put into the calculator by that number. If he says 4 is his favorite number, for example, tell him to multiply by 12. If he says 7, he needs to multiply by 21. What he'll get is an answer that's a row of his favorite number.

The Three-Dice Trick. You need three dice as well as your magic calculator. Get someone in the audience to roll the dice. You, with the help of your calculator, will guess the three numbers that came up. After the dice are rolled, give someone the calculator and give these instructions:

1. Multiply the number on one of the dice by 2.

2. Add 5.

3. Multiply this result by 5.

4. Add a number from one of the other two dice.

5. Now multiply by 10.

6. Add the third number.

7. Give back the calculator.

You subtract 250. There will be a three-digit number. The three digits will be the numbers that came up on the dice.

106

The Guess-the-Card Trick. Ask someone to pick any card from the deck. Everyone should see it except for you. Your job is to guess that card, with the help of your magic calculator. Give the person who picked the card the calculator and give these directions:

1. Punch in the card number (ace = 1, jack = 11, queen = 12, king = 13).

2. Multiply that number by 2.

3. Add 1.

4. Multiply by 5.

5. Add another number depending on which suit the card is: clubs = 6, diamonds = 7, hearts = 8, spades = 9.

6. Ask to see the calculator with the answer showing.

Whatever number is now on the calculator, subtract 5 from it. The tens place of your final answer tells the number of the card. The ones place tells the suit according to the numbers above.

Here's an example: Let's suppose someone picks the 8 of clubs. Eight is punched in. Multiply it by 2 for 16. Adding 1 gives 17. Multiply by 5 for 85. Add six since it's a club, and that brings the number to 91. The calculator shows 91. You subtract 5 and get 86. The 8 is the number of the card; the 6 tells you that it's a club. Presto!

Getting Your Money's Worth

Which would you rather have: your weight in dimes or your weight in half dollars? Would you make the same choice if you were offered a barrel of dimes or a barrel of half dollars if both barrels were the same size?

Answers to *Cross-Country Traveling:*
1-g, 5-q, 3-c, 4-p, 2-t, e-6

The Magic Touch

This card trick requires that you wear something with a pocket large enough to hold a deck of cards. Here's how the trick looks to the audience. Someone shuffles the cards, which you put into your pocket. Then you ask someone to name any one card from the deck. Suppose the 6 of diamonds is named. You reach into your pocket and take out a card that is a diamond, checking with the audience to see that you have the right suit. Then you reach in again and pull out a 4 and a 2 and ask if the sum of these two is the same as the chosen card. What a touch!

one with the correct suit. Suppose this time the card named was the jack of spades. You've already drawn out the 8 of spades to show the suit. Now you need to pull out the cards that add up to 11: ace, 2, and 8 do it. You already have the 8, so pull out the ace and 2 and you tell the audience to total all three cards to get the correct number. If it had been the jack of hearts that had been named, you wouldn't need the 4 of hearts after you used it to show the suit. In that case you just discard it and pull out the other three. Once in a while, someone will name one of the four magic cards, then you really show some magic.

Do 4 and 2 add up to the chosen card?

Neat.

Where does he get these tricks?

To get ready for this trick remove four cards from the deck before you give it to the audience and put these four in your pocket in an order that you have memorized. The four cards are the ace of clubs, the 2 of diamonds, the 4 of hearts, and the 8 of spades. In this order the numbers go from smallest to largest and the suits are in alphabetical order. The order isn't important, as long as you can reach in and pull out any one you want at any time. Practice this ahead of time.

Now, when the deck is shuffled, put it in your pocket without disturbing the four cards already there. When you're told the card, reach in and pick out the

These cards go in your pocket beforehand.

What about the four secret cards? Having one of each suit is essential for being able to pull out the correct suit. But why the ace, 2, 4, and 8? That's because you can make any number up to 15 by adding different combinations of those four numbers. Here's a chart that shows how. A checkmark indicates that a number is being used.

8	4	2	1	
			✓	1
		✓		2
		✓	✓	3
	✓			4
	✓		✓	5
	✓	✓		6
	✓	✓	✓	7
✓				8
✓			✓	9
✓		✓		10
✓		✓	✓	11
✓	✓			12
✓	✓		✓	13

These are the only four numbers that will work. Notice that each one is a double of the one smaller than it is, two times as large. Mathematicians call these numbers the "powers of two."

Answer to King Arthur's Problem: Certainly, one number is the 976 at 5 976 962.

★ $1 SENTENCE ★

Kristen imported raincoats wholesale.

Answer to *Who's Who?*:

Joshua is 11, and Rachel is 13. Marie is 9 years old, Mark is 10.

Here's the answer to **Quick Change**.

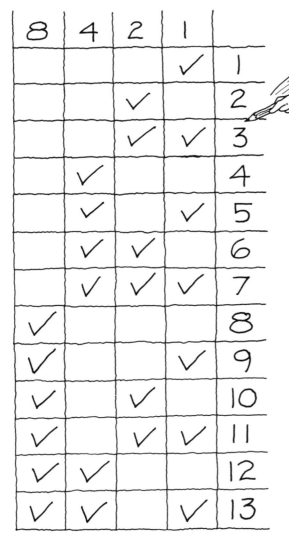

The Force Is with You

Here's another mathemagic trick you can perform for several friends. Give them each a slip of paper and ask them to write their names on one side. Collect the papers.

Then ask each of them to think of a number from 51 to 100. Tell them to concentrate on the numbers they've chosen so you can get their thoughts.

Ask them to concentrate quietly so "the force" can be with you. While they're doing this, you write a number on each of their slips of paper, on the blank side, and then fold them so only their names are showing.

When you have done this, tell them to each add a certain number you give them to their own. You give the same number to all of them. Then they each cross out the left-hand digit in their answer and add that digit to what's left of the number. When you hand each of them the folded paper with their name on it, the number they now have is written inside.

How can you be so clever? Well, first of all, they'll all wind up with the same answer. The mathemagic takes care of that. Writing the numbers on different slips of paper just adds to their amazement.

Here's what you do. Pick a number from 1 to 50 that you'd like them all to finally get and write that on each slip. In your head subtract your number from 99. Say the result out loud. That's the number they add to their thought number. Suppose you picked 26 and wrote that on their slips of paper. Subtract 26 from 99 and you get 73. They each add 73 to their number.

Suppose someone picked the number 65. Adding 73 gives 138. Cross out the left-hand digit, the 1, and add that to what's left, the 38. That gives 39. Subtract 39 from the original 65, and that leaves 26, the number you've already written. If you suspect that some in your audience might not be too terrific in arithmetic, have them work in pairs, each pair giving you one slip. (Or let them borrow your magic calculator.) The real force, of course, is mathematics!

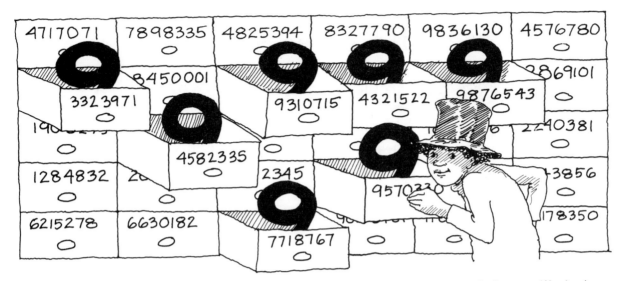

You Always Get Nine

Take any number at all, with as many digits as you like. (Your telephone number is as good as any to start with.) Write down your number. Then scramble those digits any way you'd like.

Subtract the smaller from the larger of these two numbers. Whatever answer you get, add up the digits in it. And whatever sum you get from this, add those digits again. And keep adding them until you wind up with just one number. It will be a 9.

Here's an example. Suppose you start with 4572738. Rearrange them to this: 8747523. Subtract: 8747523 - 4574738 = 4174785. Add up those digits: 4 + 1 + 7 + 4 + 7 + 8 + 5. That sum is 36. And add the 3 and the 6; you get 9.

This will work every time. It doesn't matter what number you start with. It doesn't matter how you rearrange them. Add this to your collection of mathemagic.

★ $1 SENTENCE ★

Thirty costumed starfish merrily performed.

Metric Eyesight

Having 20-20 vision means that your eyes are in great shape. A person with 20-20 vision can read a certain line on an eye chart that is placed 20 feet away. What's going to happen in the eye doctor's office when the metric system takes over?

The Three Sacks

The three little pig eyes have a few standard tricks to fall back on when things get a bit slow. This does happen to them from time to time. It's one of the regular patterns of life as a trickster. (If you have never heard of the three little pig eyes and are wondering what this is all about, you may want to check the tale on page 22 for a proper introduction to this strange trio.)

The three little pig eyes always keep their eyes open (as wide as they can, that is) for fairs and carnivals. Being magical creatures, it's easy for them to sneak in, open a booth, and not be noticed as being strange. Well, at least not *too* strange.

One of their favorite booths to set up at fairs and carnivals is the three sacks booth. It's quick and simple. They have three sacks of things and charge people to guess what's in each. The people who guess right get a prize.

Here's one they set up last summer at a carnival. Their sign was a real grabber: Pay a nickel to win a quarter! Increase your 5 cents by 500 percent.

T.J. was one of the customers who got interested. One trickster explained to him what was in the three sacks: "Money, money, they're full of money. There are nickels and quarters, and I'm not being funny." Then it pointed to the sacks and continued the rhyme, "One sack has quarters; another has nickels; the third sack, however, is really a tickle. It's a mixture of both, a fair share of each; finding which sack is which is within your reach." (The pig eyes never claimed to be great poets.)

This got T.J. interested, but he was also pretty confused. You see, each of the sacks was clearly labeled. One was labeled "Nickels"; one was labeled "Quarters"; and the third was labeled "Nickels and Quarters." So it seemed like no problem at all to find out which sack was which. But you must remember that the three little pig eyes are tricky creatures, and things are rarely as they seem when you are around them.

At this point, with T.J. even more interested, another of the pig eyes explained further. "The labels aren't right," this trickster said. "It wouldn't be much of a trick if you just paid your nickel and told us which sack had which coins in it and then got a quarter. We'd be out of quarters in no time."

T.J. was willing. "I'll take a chance," he said. The three little pig eyes snapped into action.

"That will be one nickel, please," one pig eyes said.

Then another explained, "One clue is that each of the sacks is labeled incorrectly; you can be sure about that."

That's when the third pig eyes chimed in. "But we don't expect you merely to guess. We give you clues. Two clues. And with the two clues, you can definitely figure out which sack is which—with some clever thinking, that is."

Then the third trickster finished. "You get your second clue this way: Pick any one sack, and we'll reach in and pick out one coin and show you what it is."

Which sack would you reach into?

With this explanation, T.J. decided to go for it. Then he got the details of the problem. "I've got two and a half dozen coins," one of the pig eyes said slyly. "All totaled, I've got 32 cents. What are the coins?"

T.J. won. (Actually, people won pretty often. Especially the ones who were math smarty pants.) So then the little pig eyes, tricksters that they were, came up with another offer. It went something like this.

"Say," one of them said to T.J., "would you like a chance to double your winnings?"

"How?" T.J. asked.

"It's another problem. I tell you how many coins I have in my pocket and how much they're worth all together. If you can figure out what the coins are, I'll give you another quarter. If not, you give me back the quarter you won."

Then to cheer up T.J., the little pig eyes gave him a riddle, for free, that he could try on someone else. They might be tricksters, but they are basically good-natured creatures. The riddle was written on a card:

Why are 1966 pennies worth almost $20?

Because 1966 pennies are worth $19.66, only 34¢ less than $20.

What am I doing here??

T.J. started to think. And think. He took out a pencil. (The pig eyes cheerfully supplied paper.) He could not figure it out, however. And he didn't feel very well when he found out what the answer was! You see, this was one of the trick questions the three little pig eyes love. It wasn't a fair-and-square problem like the three-sacks problem. This one had a trick to it. But then again, what can you expect from tricksters? Can you figure out the answer?

PART 7
Thinking Big

You see, according to this, no number will ever be considered a big number. It will just be 1 more than the one before it. That proves it.

968,321,055 · 968,321,056

There's something wrong here. It's logical, but it's not right. I know it's just not right.

968,321,0 5 56

Sally's reasoning may seem logical, but Boots is right. Sally isn't correct. Numbers can be big, too big to imagine even. Take one million, for example. A million of something is really too large to imagine. If this entire book were filled with words, with no pictures at all, there wouldn't be a million words in it. Not even a million letters. Not even half a million letters. So there's something wrong with Sally's reasoning. Can you figure out what it is? Maybe this chapter will help.

I say Sally's been hanging around those pig eyes too much.

How Big Is Big?

Suppose you tried to count to 1,000,000 and counted just one number each second, without taking out any time for eating or sleeping or even practicing the piano. How long would it take? A calculator helps to figure out this one. Start like this: There are 60 seconds in a minute, and 60 minutes in an hour, so that makes 3,600 seconds in an hour. There are 24 hours in a day, which means there are 86,400 seconds in a day. You take it from there.

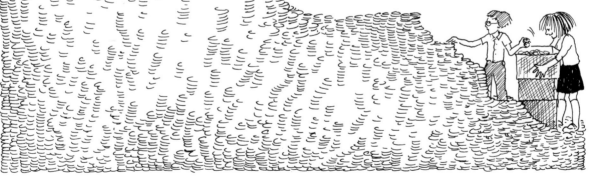

Students in Sherwood Bates Elementary School in Raleigh, North Carolina, were learning what 1,000,000 looked like firsthand, at least in bottle caps. They started collecting bottle caps in September. By March they had 787,000, which meant almost a quarter of a million still to go. That's when a snag developed. What were they going to do with all those bottle caps? Already what they had collected would fill about 150 *large* boxes!

The Sherwood Bates students finally made it, with a grand total of more than 1,170,000 bottle caps. And North Carolina solved their problem of what to do with the caps—they bought them for recycling. The Mayor of Raleigh declared June 13, 1980, as Bank-a-Million Day.

What about 1,000,000 days? How many years would that be? Will you be alive a million days from now?

Would 1,000,000 pennies fit in your bedroom? One million pennies weigh over 3 tons. Could your bedroom hold that weight? (How much are 1,000,000 pennies worth anyway?)

If you had a cylindrical tank big enough to hold 1,000,000 glasses of milk, it would need to be 75 feet high and 10 feet in diameter.

Can you imagine how big 1,000,000 really is?

Mathematical Abbreviations

To write one million as a numeral takes a 1 and six 0's: 1,000,000. To write one billion, you use a 1 and nine 0's: 1,000,000,000. One trillion uses three more 0's: 1,000,000,000,000.

Large numbers have always been interesting to mathematicians. Writing lots of zeros isn't so interesting. There's a way to write abbreviations for large numbers, without all those zeros. One million (1,000,000) can be written 10^6. One billion (1,000,000,000) is 10^9. One trillion (1,000,000,000,000) is 10^{12}. The little number is the same as the number of zeros, and is called an "exponent." An exponent tells how many times to multiply the other number, called the "base," by itself. So 10^6 equals 10 x 10 x 10 x 10 x 10 x 10, and that equals 1,000,000. (You can check that on your calculator.)

$$100 = 10^2 (10 \times 10)$$
$$1,000 = 10^3 (10 \times 10 \times 10)$$
$$10,000 = 10^4 (10 \times 10 \times 10 \times 10)$$
$$100,000 = 10^5 (10 \times 10 \times 10 \times 10 \times 10)$$

All of these numbers are called "powers of ten." To read any one of them, such as 1,000, you can say "one thousand," or "ten to the third power." One million is "ten to the sixth power."

With numbers that aren't exactly a power of ten, 13 million (13,000,000), for example, mathematicians use a short-hand that still uses exponents with ten as the base. Since 13 million is 13 times 1 million, you can write it as 13 x 10^6. That's a standard abbreviation called "scientific notation." You'll probably run across this in school sometime, if you haven't already. Remember, an abbreviation is useful to you only if you understand where it came from and what it means!

More Mathematical Abbreviations

Exponents are especially useful when the powers of ten get even bigger. Here's a chart that shows how handy mathematical shorthand can be.

Power of Ten	Number name
10^3	Thousand
10^6	Million
10^9	Billion
10^{12}	Trillion
10^{15}	Quadrillion
10^{18}	Quintillion
10^{21}	Sextillion
10^{24}	Septillion
10^{27}	Octillion
10^{30}	Nonillion
10^{33}	Decillion
10^{36}	Undecillion
10^{39}	Duodecillion
10^{42}	Tredecillion
10^{45}	Quattuordecillion
10^{48}	Quindecillion
10^{51}	Sexdecillion
10^{54}	Septendecillion
10^{57}	Octodecillion
10^{60}	Novemdecillion
10^{63}	Vigintillion
10^{100}	Googol

Can you figure out what number name fits 10^8? Or 10^{10}?

Which Is Bigger? One million billion or one billion million? Can you write each of these as a power of ten?

Answers to the *Pizza Problems*:
#1: The time would be a quarter to two. #2: The other half.
#3: He was not hungry enough to eat eight pieces. #4: Cut it in half. Stack the two halves on top of each other. Cut this pile in half again. Now you have four pieces. Stack them on top of each other and cut in half again.
#5: Alicia's favorite pizza is mushroom. Mike's is sausage. Patrick's is anchovy and Susan's is pepperoni! #6: There are 105 different pizzas with two ingredients each. #7: Ten minutes.

Powers Other Than Ten

You don't have to use exponents just for powers of ten. You can have powers of two, three, or of any number. The rule is still the same: The exponent tells how many times to multiply the base by itself. So 2^6 means $2 \times 2 \times 2 \times 2 \times 2 \times 2$, which is 64. And 6^2 means 6×6, or 36.

Which of these pairs is more?

2^3 or 3^2

2^4 or 4^2

2^5 or 5^2

Do you notice a pattern about these? Is that pattern true for other bases and exponents?

The Fifth Powers. It has been said that the fifth power of a number always ends in the last digit of the base number. For example, $2^5 = 32$ and $13^5 = 371,293$. Test this for others.

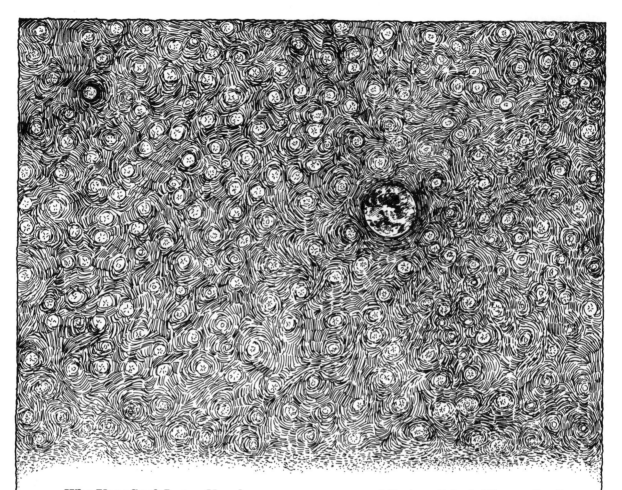

Who Uses Such Large Numbers Anyway?

If such large numbers are so hard to imagine, why bother with them? For some people they're very important. Astronomers, for example. You may have learned about the speed of light in school; light travels at 186,000 miles per second. The sun is 93,000,000 miles away from Earth (more or less—at that distance a few miles doesn't make much difference). So it takes the light from the sun about 8 minutes to reach the Earth.

How far does light travel in 1 year? There are 86,400 seconds in 1 day, and just about 365¼ days in a year. So in 1 year, light travels 186,000 x 86,400 x 365¼ miles. This is about 6,000,000,000,-000 (6×10^{12}) miles (more or less). You can read that as "six trillion miles" or "six times ten to the twelfth power miles." But instead of either of those, that distance is called "one light year." Can you explain why?

A light year is an incredibly long distance, much too long to visualize. But scientists know that many stars are much farther away from Earth than that, and that a light year really isn't so terribly far when you're thinking about the universe. Polaris is the North Star, the one at the end of the handle of the Little Dipper. It is 300 light years away from Earth. That means that on any night you're looking at that star, the light you see is the way Polaris looked 300 years ago! Some of the stars you see at night don't even exist anymore; they've already died, but their light is just now getting to Earth.

A Speedy Problem

For this problem you need to know two speeds. Light travels fast: 186,000 miles per second. Sound travels fast, but not as fast: 1,100 feet per second.

Suppose you're at a rock concert, sitting 100 feet from the band. The concert is being broadcast on the radio, and someone is listening to it 1,000 miles away. Radio waves travel at the speed of light. Who will hear the music first—you or the radio listener?

Worldwide News

Suppose a baby was born at midnight, and you told one person about this new baby. Then that person told two others within 10 minutes. And then those two each told two others in 10 minutes. And this continued all night long, with every person telling two others every 10 minutes who hadn't yet been told. How many people would know by 8 o'clock in the morning?

Answers to *The Three Sacks*: The correct sack to reach into is the one labeled "Nickels and Quarters." You knew that. But with the second problem, I did not figure out that there were two pennies and six nickels in the big ones, pocket the six nickels, make the fifth dozen coins in the problem, and the two pennies were the other two. See, it was a trick question.

The Million-Dollar Giveaway

If you had $1,000,000 (don't you wish?), and you decided to give away $50 every hour, how long would it take you to give away the total amount? How old would you be then?

Math on the Beach. If you look at a 1-mile stretch of beach that is 100 feet wide and 1 foot deep, you're looking at 10^{14} grains of sand. That's one hundred trillion, and nothing to sneeze at.

Some Numbers Are
More Perfect Than Others

I'm sure *they* realized the error of their ways. Euclid, that dear boy, one of the most spectacular of the Greeks, wrote about me and some of my perfect friends in the first century B.C. He appreciated us, not only because we are so perfect, but because he knew how rare we are.

It was no easy task to find us. After me comes 28. And the third comes a long way after; it's 496. The fourth is 8,128. It took mathematicians over 1,500 years to find the fifth perfect number. It was a toughie, a real hide-out: 33,550,336. And it has only been since the invention of the electronic computing machines that they have found the next one: 8,589,869,056. Oh, we're a rare collection. (But I'm first and always will be.)

Being perfect isn't easy, I'll have you know. It's hard to find friends of my quality. After all, there just aren't too many perfect numbers around. I'm the smallest of all of us; and I was the first one discovered. The Greeks found me, for which I'm grateful. Deeply grateful.

Those Greeks were extraordinary fellows. They felt that we perfect numbers are rather mystical. Some felt we were slightly nonsensical as well, but

I'm sure you're wondering what makes us so very perfect. It has to do with our proper divisors, you see, the numbers which are smaller than we are and divide into us evenly. For each of us absolutely perfect numerical wonders, our proper divisors add up to us, exactly. Take me for instance. My proper divisors are 1, 2, and 3. (Not 4, or 5, since they don't divide into me evenly. I've always detested leftovers.) And if you add 1, 2, and 3, you get me, 6. It's just perfect.

That simply marvelous property doesn't occur again until 28. The divisors of 28 are 1, 2, (not 3), 4, (not 5 or 6), 7, and 14. Just those five. You can check for yourself that they add up to 28.

If you're one of those doubting types (and I certainly hope you are—doubters are so much more exciting as thinkers), check out 496.

I was at a party recently. I can't remember where the party was—I'm invited to *so* many. Well, there was a 10 just preening for a group of admirers.

"What's going on here?" I whispered to a friend.

"Well," she said, "they all think that 10 is absolutely perfect. After all, it has done so much for place value and is a perfect match for people's fingers and toes."

"What?" I said, a bit louder than I had meant to, I'm afraid. Well, I just couldn't contain myself. This was an impostor of the worst sort. Now 10 may have some interesting characteristics (though I've never really noticed them myself), but being perfect is definitely not one of them. Even the mathematicians agree. Check its perfect divisors for yourself. The only numbers smaller than 10 that divide into it evenly are 1, 2, and 5. Add those and all you get is 8.

Hardly 10. And when a number's proper divisors add up to less than itself, it's given a most appropriate label. The mathematicians call those numbers "deficient," and I agree with them wholeheartedly.

Now there are some numbers that aren't perfect, but they aren't deficient either. Take 12, for example. Its proper divisors are 1, 2, 3, 4, and 6. Add those up, and you get a hefty sum: 16. (Some numbers have just let themselves go.) "Abundant" is what mathematicians call these numbers, a rather polite label for such chubby entities.

We perfect numbers have dazzled mathematicians for ages. For example, they've noticed that all of us are even. Well, of course! What did you expect? But those mathematicians are doubters. Darlings, but doubters. They like to prove things, and they've been trying for simply ages to prove that an odd number can't be perfect, but none of them has done it yet! They just don't come like Euclid anymore!

Before I go, dear readers, I have a question for you. How old are you? Is your age perfect or abundant or deficient?

And one more thing — *if you can imagine this at all* — the seventeenth perfect number has 1,373 digits in it! Talk about perfection!

126

MATH TALK

In mathematics, easy words sometimes stand for not-so-easy ideas. And that can be confusing. You know the words, but you don't necessarily know what the mathematical meanings for them are.

Take the word "perfect" for an example. Think about what the word perfect means to you. Check it in the dictionary. Now can you see any reason why the number 28 ought to be called perfect? Check page 124 to find out. It doesn't have much to do with what "perfect" means in a nonmathematical sense.

If you feel positive, or negative, about something, that's a sign of your attitude. Not so in mathematics. Positive and negative numbers aren't cheerful or grumpy. Positive numbers are larger than zero, and negative numbers are smaller than zero, and that's all there is to that.

An odd number isn't terribly unusual, it just isn't even. Hardly enough excuse to be called odd in English, but perfectly understandable in mathematics!

There are other such words: table, plot, function, product, times, power. And lots more. It's as if some words have one meaning in English and an entirely different meaning in mathematics.

Some of learning mathematics has to do with understanding ideas that have names similar to other, unrelated ideas. You need to remember that. And you need to remember that the *ideas* are the important things. The names are only as useful to you as your understanding of them.

★

Read the following description and see if you can figure out what is being described. It's an object that is usually found in homes where someone sews.

> A portion of a small right circular cone, made by a cut parallel to its base, convex on the crown, semiperforated with symmetrical indentations, usually congruent with a hollow interior.

It's a thimble. Aren't you glad mathematicians don't run everything in this world?

Books and Islands in Ojibwe Country

LOUISE ERDRICH

Books and Islands in Ojibwe Country

NATIONAL GEOGRAPHIC DIRECTIONS

NATIONAL GEOGRAPHIC
Washington, D.C.

Published by the National Geographic Society
1145 17th Street, N.W., Washington, DC 20036-4688

Text and illustrations copyright © 2003 Louise Erdrich
Map © 2003 National Geographic Society

Drawings by the author

Library of Congress Cataloging-in-Publication Data

Erdrich, Louise.
    Books and islands in Ojibwe country / Louise Erdrich
        p. cm. -- (National Geographic directions)
    ISBN: 0-7922-5719-7
        1. Ojibwa Indians. 2. Erdrich, Louise. 3. Lake of the Woods. 4. Novelists,
American--20th century--Biography. I. Title. II. Series

E99.C6E63 2003
977.004'973--dc21

                                                                2003045906

One of the world's largest nonprofit scientific and educational organizations, the National Geographic Society was founded in 1888 "for the increase and diffusion of geographic knowledge." Fulfilling this mission, the Society educates and inspires millions every day through its magazines, books, television programs, videos, maps and atlases, research grants, the National Geographic Bee, teacher workshops, and innovative classroom materials. The Society is supported through membership dues, charitable gifts, and income from the sale of its educational products. This support is vital to National Geographic's mission to increase global understanding and promote conservation of our planet through exploration, research, and education.

For more information, please call 1-800-NGS LINE (647-5463), write to the Society at the above address, or visit the Society's Web site at www.nationalgeographic.com.

Interior design by Michael Ian Kaye and Tuan Ching, Ogilvy & Mather, Brand Integration Group

Printed in the U.S.A.

for Nenaa'ikiizhikok
and her brothers and sisters

.

CONTENTS

Books and Islands in Ojibwe Country

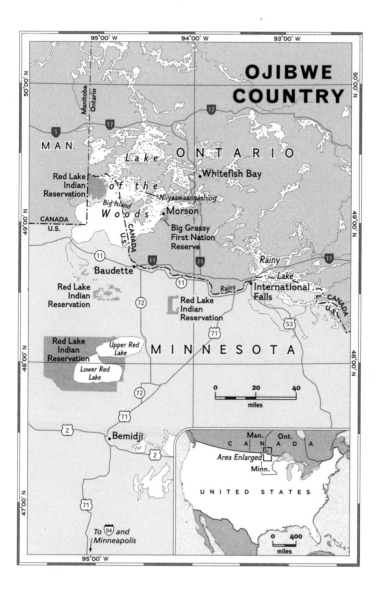

OJIBWE COUNTRY

MAN.

ONTARIO

Lake

of the

Woods

Red Lake
Indian
Reservation

Big Island

CANADA
U.S.

•Whitefish Bay

Niiyaawaangashing

•Morson

Big Grassy
First Nation
Reserve

Rainy

•Baudette

Red Lake
Indian
Reservation

Red Lake
Indian
Reservation

Upper Red
Lake

Lower Red
Lake

MINNESOTA

Lake

Rainy

International
Falls

CANADA
U.S.

0   20   40
miles

•Bemidji

To 94 and
Minneapolis

CANADA

Man. | Ont.

Area Enlarged

Minn.

UNITED STATES

0   400
miles

CHAPTER ONE

Books and Islands

My travels have become so focused on books and islands that the two have merged for me. Books, islands. Islands, books. Lake of the Woods in Ontario and Minnesota has 14,000 islands. Some of them are painted islands, the rocks bearing signs ranging from a few hundred to more than a thousand years old. So these islands, which I'm longing to read, are books in themselves. And then there is a special island on Rainy Lake that is home to thousands of rare books ranging from crumbling copies of Erasmus in the French and Heloise's letters to Abelard dated MDCCXXIII, to first editions of Mark Twain (signed) to a magnificent collection of ethnographic works on the Ojibwe that might help explain the book-islands of Lake of the Woods.

I am not traveling alone. First my eighteen-month-old and still nursing daughter and I will pop over the Canada-U.S. border and visit Lake of the Woods and the lands of her namesake, her grandmother. Then we'll dip below the border and travel east to Rainy Lake. We'll put about a thousand miles on our car and several hundred on other people's boats. I'm forty-eight years old and I can't travel aimlessly. I always seem to have a question that I would like to answer. Increasingly, too, it is the same question. It is the question that has defined my life, the question that has saved my life, and the question that most recently has resulted in the questionable enterprise of starting a bookstore. The question is: Books. Why? The islands are really incidental. I'm not much

in favor of them. I grew up on the Great Plains. I'm a dry-land-for-hundreds-of-miles person, but I've gotten mixed up with people who live on lakes. And then these islands have begun to haunt me, especially the one with all of the books.

Mazina'iganan is the word for "books" in Ojibwemowin or Anishinabemowin, and *mazinapikiniganan* is the word for "rock paintings." Ojibwemowin is the Algonquin language originally spoken by the Ojibwe people living throughout Michigan, Minnesota, Ontario, Manitoba, and on into North Dakota. As you can see, both words begin with "mazina." It is the root for dozens of words all concerned with made images and with the substances upon which the images are put, mainly paper or screens. As the Ojibwe people began to watch television and go to movies, the word came in handy. *Mazinaatesewigamig.* Movie Theater. *Mazinatesijigan.* Television set. They had a root word ready to make into a verb way back when Edward Curtis and later Ernest Oberholtzer came to photograph them. *Mazinaakizo.* To be photographed. (Nothing about stealing souls in the word mazinaakizo. Photographers did not take Ojibwe souls, it wasn't that easy. Soul theft required the systematic hard work of inventive humiliations and abuse by the government and by Catholic nuns and priests.)

The Ojibwe had been using the word *mazinibaganjigan* for years to describe dental pictographs made on birch-bark, perhaps the first books made in North America. Yes, I figure books have been written around here ever since someone had the idea of biting or even writing on birchbark with a sharpened stick. Books are nothing all that new. People have probably been writing books in North America since at least 2000 B.C. Or painting islands. You could think of the lakes as libraries. 2000 B.C.

is only the date of the oldest archaeological evidence people left in the area we are going to visit. Traditional Anishinaabe people find the land-bridge theory a concept convenient to non-Indians and insist they've been here forever. And in truth, since the writing or drawings that those ancient people left still makes sense to people living in Lake of the Woods today, one must conclude that they weren't the ancestors of the modern Ojibwe. They were and are the modern Ojibwe.

Books. Why?

Because our brains hurt.

How A Mother Packs

For a week before I leave on any trip, I am distracted and full of cares. Just at the last minute, I always find myself doing things that I have put off for months, even years. I always change my will, then clean out cabinets and file old letters. I make certain that we all have sufficient underwear, that money and phone numbers are in relevant hands, the dog's vaccinated for Lyme disease, the manuscript of the last book is in production, the baby has her shots. Then I get more specific to the trip itself. I read books on pictographs and decide which notebooks to take along. Change the oil in the car. Make sure that my older daughters have postcards and shampoo. I buy tobacco— not to smoke but to offer to the spirits of the lake and the spirits of the rock paintings we will visit. I gather gifts for the paintings—a ribbon shirt, some red cloth, sage bundles. I purchase 124 disposable diapers and one of those baby harnesses I see mothers using in malls. If the baby goes over the edge of a boat or off an island, I picture myself hauling her right up. I go over plans for housesitting and financial reports and make certain that our bookstore doesn't need me. There are so many small things. It is the small things that will consume me. The sunblock. The elms that must be treated with fungicide. The shoes. The many sizes and types of shoes girls wear all through their lives. I tell myself that God and meaning are in the small things as well as in the vast. But where in the wilderness of shoes is God? In the laces? The rubber bumpers? The heels that swiftly rise at age twelve?

On the other hand, none of this matters at all. The attention to details is just a way to stave off facing the truth. I hate leaving home.

Home

My 103-year-old house is surrounded by great trees. I have named each one of them. There is Guarding Elm that leans and tosses to the west, just beyond the blue gate. Tiny Offshoot of the Great Wahpeton Maple grows alongside, only six feet tall. It is still shaped like a drumstick. I grew it from a seedling that took root in one of my mother's flowerpots. Awkward and Shy are the elms that flank these two trees and Old Stalwart, biggest tree in the neighborhood, stands guard around the corner, in front of the house. Pensive Lover and Serene Darling, Haywire and Entire Trust are the locust trees that have sprung up in a ragged line along the edge of the yard. I have great admiration for these trees as they seem unkillable and their fronds of tossing leaves provide an ever shifting and trembling pattern of shadows on the old cream-colored walls inside our house. Also, they leaf out last of all and lose their leaves last, too, every fall, providing one final bank of burnished glory before the blastoff into winter.

Our house was built as a wedding gift for a father's much adored daughter. His house, same layout, still stands next door. This house was built when the lake to our east was still a marsh, before it was dredged. Our house even looks a bit like a wedding cake, trimmed with spindle rails, bows carved over the window, egg and dart molding, and a couple of round peephole windows. Perhaps one day we'll attach a cheesy fifteen-foot plastic bride and groom to the roof. During the sixties, our house was gutted and became a rooming house, then a duplex. The interior lost its charming details and became just peculiar. Guests have seen a ghost on the top floor and the girls hear it walking. They believe he is a confused man, and that's what we call him. Sometimes, when one of my older daughters is gone for a while, the baby and I will sleep in her room so that the ghost of The Confused Man does not take up residence.

I describe all of this because there can be no traveling unless there is a leave-taking. And the traveling is all the more in earnest if the leaving is difficult. For me, leaving hurts. This is the dwelling of four essential beings. My daughters. Even when they are not here, all of their things are here. We don't mean to become attached to things, but we do and rather than live in complete clutter, we are always culling, throwing, giving.

We have a lot of books in our house. They are our primary decorative motif—books in piles on the coffee table, framed book covers, books sorted into stacks on every available surface, and of course books on shelves along most walls. Besides the visible books, there are the boxes waiting in the wings, the basement books, the garage books, the storage locker books. They are a sort of insulation, soundproofing some walls. They function as furniture, they prop up sagging fixtures and disguised by quilts function as tables. The quantities and types of books are fluid, arriving like hysterical cousins in overnight shipping envelopes only to languish near the overflowing mail bench. Advance Reading Copies collect at bedside, to be dutifully examined—to ignore them and read Henry James or Barbara Pym instead becomes a guilty pleasure. I can't imagine home without an overflow of books. The point of books is to have way too many but to always feel you never have enough, or the right one at the right moment, but then sometimes to find you'd longed to fall asleep reading *The Aspern Papers,* and there it is.

Books. Another reason. I can take home along any-where in the person of a book, and I do. I pack W. G. Sebald's *Austerlitz*. I bring Jim Crace's *Quarantine* and *Being Dead*. Then I add *Saints and Strangers* by Angela Carter, and *The Stone Diaries* by Carol Shields, which everybody else has read. That takes care of fiction. As for nonfiction, I never go anywhere without *A Concise Dictionary of Minnesota Ojibwe*, John D. Nichols and Earl Nyholm. I take along Joe Paddock's book on Ernest Oberholtzer, *Keeper of the Wild*. And then I pack a bag containing all of my baby's books, many of which I've laboriously blotted with Wite-Out, removing the English, and replaced with Ojibwe words written in Magic Marker.

Ojibwe

Ojibwe is also slurred into the word Chippewa and in its original form, Anishinaabe, it is pronounced Ah-NISH-in-AH-bay. The word is very loaded and bears a host of meanings and interpretations and theories. I've heard that Ojibwe refers to the puckering of the seams of traditional moccasins, or *makazinan*. Or that the Ojibwe roasted their enemies "until they puckered up." Gruesome. I've heard that Anishinaabe means "from whence is lowered the male of the species," but I don't like that one very much. And then there is the more mystical Spontaneous Beings. The meaning that I like best of course is Ojibwe from the verb

Ozhibii'ige, which is "to write." Ojibwe people were great writers from way back and synthesized the oral and written tradition by keeping mnemonic scrolls of inscribed birchbark. The first paper, the first books.

The Blue Minivan

I am connected to and believe in my 1995 blue Windstar Minivan. We have history. I know exactly how to pack this vehicle, and feel its personality is with me as I fill the crevices between, under, behind the blue cloth seats. The blue Windstar is sisterly, accommodating, personable. And a gallant hauler. Used to be, I'd pack six preteen girls, two dogs (large Aussies), and myself in along with a week of food, clothes, games, and drawing materials, for a trip to a whole other island in Lake Superior where I did research while the girls swam, screamed, ate, screamed, roasted marshmallows, screamed, read "Wonder Woman" and "Catwoman" comics, slept, screamed, and woke, screaming happily, for a week or two. I don't really know how I have accomplished anything, ever. The minivan has been to North Dakota many times to visit Wahpeton, where my parents live, and to South Dakota, bearing my favorite sun dancer, my baby's father. With the backseats removed, he could sleep comfortably on a futon. The Windstar came back a little bloodstained, loaded with slabs of pipestone, great barrel-sized bundles of sage, a small prayer flag tied to its antenna. It made a traveling home for the sun dancer, the man whom we'll soon meet, who was named after low-lying clouds over the water of the lake we are going to visit.

Nenaa'ikiizhikok

This is what I have been told. There are four spirit women who take care of all of the waters of the world. One woman cares for the oceans of salt water. A second woman cares for the freshwater lakes, streams, and rivers. Yet a third woman cares for the waters inside of women that surround and cushion their babies. The fourth woman looks after the rains, the clouds, the storms, the waters in the sky. That woman cleans the sky up after a thunderstorm, makes sure the clouds are moving. The stars properly fixed in their places. She's always hard at work healing and arranging the sky so that things flow in the right order and direction. The baby in the car seat directly behind me is named for that spirit woman, Nenaa'ikiizhikok. Her grandmother on her father's side had this name, and was called Kiizhikok, Sky Woman, or Kiizhik; Sky, for short.

The original Nenaa'ikiizhikok was an imposing woman, tall and strikingly intelligent. The only image I have of her is from the back row of a boarding school class picture. She's blurred, of course, but obviously beautiful—

not pretty—her features are too strong and cunning for merely pretty. This Nenaa'ikiizhikok is spoken of in Ojibwemowin as Nenaa'ikiizhikokiban. The "iban" at the end puts her in the past, in the spirit world, where I imagine she is still dancing in her jingle dress. She was a well-known expert jingle-dress dancer, and even came to the Turtle Mountains to powwow. My mother, Rita Gourneau Erdrich, grew up in the Turtle Mountains. My family is still there so I visit as often as I can. I like to imagine Nenaa'ikiizhikokiban dancing with one of my mother's aunts, maybe Jane or Shyoosh.

Baby Nenaa'ikiizhikok also has my mother's name, Rita. So she's a grandmotherly little baby, I guess. She even has one gray hair growing on the back of her head. I'm old to be a new mother of course, and so's her dad. Our baby was born a great-aunt. But we won't get into that. As my brother Ralph says, a look of distress on his face, "Don't say anymore about it! I knew she'd be something like a *great-aunt* already! I just don't want to know!"

Right now Kiizhikok is playing with her baby cell phone.

The plastic cell phone keeps saying "yellow triangle." It is a teaching cell phone. She drops it and picks up her teaching hammer. It says, "Can we fix it? Yes, we can!" She drops it, and picks up a musical box that lights up and plays bits of Mozart and Bach. She drops that and picks up a bright baby tape recorder that plays her late great-uncle Kwekwekibiness singing the Lake of the Woods song, which was given to the people in dreams by the lake itself. Eventually, she turns that off. Eats a cracker. As befits a child born with a gray hair, she is a very philosophical baby, personable and good-natured. She fusses for perhaps five minutes. Sleeps for two hours as we travel along a highway that was expanded from a road that was once a trail, an old Ojibwe trade route, heading north.

Songs traveled this route, and ceremonies, as well as pelts and guns. Medicines, knowledge, sacred shells, and secular ideas traveled this road, but never at sixty-five miles per hour. The van is kind, the van is good. She's got new brake pads and an alignment. She'll get us there.

Asema, Age, and Gratitude

The word for "tobacco" is *asema,* and it is essential to bring some for this reason: Spirits like tobacco. Their fondness for the stuff is a given of Ojibwe life. Tobacco offerings are made before every important request, to spirits or to other humans. Tobacco is put down by the root if you pick a plant, in the water when you visit a lake, by the side of the road when starting a journey. Tobacco is handed to anyone with whom you wish to speak in a serious manner. It is given for a story, or as an invitation to join someone in a teaching or writing project. Tobacco begins every note-worthy enterprise and is given as a thank-you at the end of every significant event. Perhaps spirits like tobacco because they like the fragrance of its smoke, or because people like tobacco and they appreciate thoughtfulness.

My grandfather made the old-time *kinnickinnick,* red willow tobacco, a smoking mixture of shaved willow bark, sage, and other local herbs. Ojibwe people still use and make red willow tobacco, but the tobacco offered these days is most often bought in pipe shops or purchased in small foil packets. Sometimes I'm offered cigarettes to help with projects or to listen to someone's problem. I quit smoking years ago. I began to cut down once I started running, for I soon realized that rolling a Bull Durham ciggie after a painful three-mile jog and puffing away to recover was counterproductive. So as I am now pure, I dismantle the cigarette, place the tobacco on the ground, then either bury or throw away the filter. My favorite tobacco comes from a pipe shop in Minneapolis

and is called Nokomis, the Ojibwe word for grandmother. It is a rich, black, softly shredded moist stuff with a darkly sweet scent. Before I take a trip like the one I am taking now, I always buy a pound or two of this tobacco and divide it into smaller bags. Some are for the baby to give to other people, and some are for the spirits of the places we're going to visit.

There was a time when I wondered—do I really believe all of this? I'm half German. Rational! Does this make any sense? After a while such questions stopped mattering. Believing or not believing, it was all the same. I found myself compelled to behave toward the world as if it contained sentient spiritual beings. The question whether or not they *actually* existed became irrelevant. After I'd stopped thinking about it for a while, the ritual of offering tobacco became comforting and then necessary. Whenever I offered tobacco I was for that moment fully there, fully thinking, willing to address the mystery.

Therefore, I've taught my children to offer tobacco (at the same time that I rail at them not to smoke it). The baby is adept at dipping her hand into the bag and waiting for the right moment to scatter the flakes. If allowed to, she'll keep offering tobacco until the bag's used up. She does it with such a sweet solemnity it's hard to stop her. *N'dawnis,* my daughter. I still am amazed to find her here.

Actually, I put down a *lot* of tobacco when I found out that I was going to have a baby. I needed every bit of spiritual help I could get. Maybe I'll get used to the fact that she is here by the time I'm sixty-four years old and clapping wildly at her high school graduation. When I walked into my midwife's office with a positive pregnancy test, one of my first questions was, "What kind of statistics are there on women who have babies at forty-seven?" Gently, I was told that statistics were unavailable because "there just aren't that many women having babies at forty-seven."

Still, I was dazzled. I felt like Mary at the Annunciation. Mary with PMS. I wept, I snarled, I laughed like a hyena. I knew that I was frightening to others, filled with a bewildering array of hormones. I'd gone from perimenopausal to violently pregnant. On the wall behind my midwife there was a framed poster of that obnoxious poem about the woman who looks forward to getting old so that she can wear purple. I happened to be wearing purple that day, and I was old, and I was pregnant. What did this mean? Along with the dazzled feeling I was struck by the awful burden of it all. How would I do it? I don't suppose the Virgin Mary felt sorry for herself, but I did. Then suddenly, I thought of a most wonderful consolation.

Books. Why?

To read and read while nursing a baby.

CHAPTER TWO

Islands

The Problem of Meeting Up in Ojibwe Country

By the end of the first day we are in Bemidji, Minnesota, home of giant replicas of Babe the Blue Ox, Paul Bunyan, and, most importantly, where my brothers live now. Louis Erdrich, named for my German grandfather, is an environmental engineer who oversees all of the systems managers throughout the northern tier of Ojibwe country down here in the United States. He is in charge of making sure that reservations all through Michigan, Wisconsin, and Minnesota have adequate water and sewage and waste disposal systems. This is a vast job, but Louis deals unflappably with toxic waste and buried gas tanks. My other brother, Ralph Erdrich, Jr., is the head emergency room nurse at Red Lake Hospital on Red Lake Reservation, just north of Bemidji. He sews up local brawlers, delivers babies, and extracts quantities of fishhooks from various parts of Red Lake Ojibwe bodies. We have some difficulty deciding where to meet for dinner, at Perkins or Country Kitchen. As we all worked at a Country Kitchen in Wahpeton, North Dakota, me as a waitress and hostess, and my brothers as cooks, there is a nostalgia factor. But as, therefore, we also know exactly what went on behind the scenes at Country Kitchen, we opt for Perkins.

The interior is crowded, steamy, loud with families. Between the two of them, my brothers have five sons and one tiny new daughter. We're sitting around three pushed-together tables, ordering baskets of onion rings and hash browns and chili and sandwiches, when I am suddenly overcome by a great feeling of happiness. My brothers are loyal and kind fellows, and they have seen me through tough times. When my husband died in 1997 they took off work to come and stay with me, to answer the telephone and guard my children. They also made sure I didn't stay in bed all day, chew the woodwork, or just sit in the corner and drool. They helped the household keep on functioning. They kept my world partly normal. They are tall and sturdy and they make me feel safe. Now, as we sit in Perkins eating deep-fried foods and dressing-drenched salads, I am again comforted by their solid presence. They don't have to be analytical, they don't have to be literary, we don't have to talk about anything at all, really. It is enough to be around them, to enjoy the continuity and the weird Erdrich history.

They are tireless professionals in their work, but sweet and nonjudgmental in their personal lives. They are what women in the Midwest call "guy guys." They do guy things like fish and watch football, refurnish furniture, and tinker with dangerous electrical wiring. In their guy-ness they relate easily to my guy, Tobasonakwut, the sun dancer and the father of Kiizhikok. They ask about him and about my plans for this trip. I am forced to say that, as usual, I have no exact idea how I'll actually meet up with him. Although, as always, I am sure it will happen.

Meeting up is always complicated in Ojibwe country, and never seems to happen as it was planned. Tobason-akwut, who is a traditional healer, as well as a tribal politician, teacher, and negotiator, is always being called on life or death missions. He has devoted his life to help-ing people. He is a one-man spiritual ER. And so, when making plans, I have found it best to be prepared to wait. I have found it best to understand things will always change and take a long time. Important and essential items will be lost, mislaid, then found, and then they will need to be repaired. I have found it best to travel with everything I need in order to spend a comfortable night, anywhere, even in my car. I spend one, though at Bemidji's Holiday Inn Express. The next morning, as soon as Kiizhikok and I have investigated the "continental breakfast" and partaken of four kinds of dried cereal, including Froot Loops, we drive straight north past Red Lake Reservation on US 72, heading for Baudette, where I'll cross the border.

I'm revved up on a cup of unfamiliar coffee. Holiday Inn Express coffee. Kiizhikok drifts off after operating a plastic blender that chimes "Old MacDonald" in the barks of dogs, the croaks of frogs, or the mews of cats, or all at once. This strangely complicated toy was made in China. I am very happy as I now get to glimpse some of my favorite country. The great *mashkiig,* or bog, between Red Lake and Lake of the Woods, is traditionally the great Ojibwe pharmacy. It is full of medicines. There is Labrador tea, or swamp tea, *makigobug.* Snakeroot, which I should be carrying for good luck and health on this journey. There is balsam, a laxative. *Ininiwunj,* or milkweed, used on whistles as a charm for drawing deer. Pitcher plant or *omukikiwidasun,* which makes great toys. The Ojibwe name means "frog leggings." There is willow for indigestion, for basketmaking, the inner bark for kinnickinnick and headaches. *Makibug,* sumac, for dysentery. White cedar for coughs. Highbush cranberry, blueberries, Juneberries, wild currants, gooseberries. *Winabojobikuk,* for snakebite. That's "Winabojo's arrow." *Winabojo nokomis winizisun,* painted cup, or "Winabojo's grandmother's hair," used for rheumatism and for the diseases of women.

One medicine I do use is a *ginebig,* or snake medicine. I've got some in a plastic baggy. Puffball powder is the spores of dried puffballs, collected from those white, round, low-growing mushrooms that grow everywhere, even on city boulevards. Put this powder on a cut or a scrape and it heals immediately. All of these medicines and countless others grow on either side of the highway in the tamarack bog, an ecosystem so vibrantly rich that traditional Ojibwe teachers and healers still go out to fast there, to show their respect for the medicines and to learn from these plants.

Red willow, stands of maple, watery alder, and birch give way at last to neat little towns and isolated farms. Up near the border, at Baudette, we buy supplies and also phone cards. The phone cards are often useless in Canada, but I buy them anyway. And then we are across the border and heading up to Morson, Ontario, through Big Grassy First Nation Reserve on a familiar little highway dotted with construction crews repairing the constant erosion and washouts. I park the blue minivan at a dock in Morson. The owner of New Moon fishing lodge, Rocky Moen, helps me unload the van and transfers the duffels, the camera equipment, the portable crib, into the lodge boat.

Rocky is a kindly and intelligent man and seems devoted to the ecology of the lake. We start talking immediately about the rock paintings as we proceed directly to the island that his family has owned since the 1950s. Rocky is intrigued with the paintings near his lodge, and he is still angry about the defacement of those paintings decades ago. "Stupid, stupid, stupid," he says. "It bothers me a lot. I know the person who did it." When I ask the person's name, though, Rocky just looks pained. The trip to the island takes about forty-five minutes, and as the mainland is blazing hot this July the cool breeze is a relief. Kiizhikok stands in the whipping wind, and I hold tightly onto the handle on the back of her life jacket and grasp one leg, too, just to make sure.

Boats make me very uncomfortable. At any moment, I think we'll ram into a rock. The boat will sink. But I'll still be gripping the baby. I'll tow her to shore. There are plenty of islands around here, and I never go out onto the lake without carrying in my pocket a Ziploc baggy of waterproof matches. Once I tow the baby to shore, I'll light a fire, fan the smoke, and eventually someone will come to investigate. We will be saved. During this short ride, I become so lost in my fantasy of boat wreck that it is only with a wrench that I return to the immediate fact that we are traveling along, so far so good, and we're not capsizing. Rocky seems completely at home on the lake. We'll probably be safe. I don't relax my grip on Kiizhikok, but I do force myself to abandon my fantasy and look around at the stunning beauty.

The islands jut from the lake, tall with hundred-year pines, rocky and severe. The water glitters with power and great tangles of second-growth bush ride by, cut with sloughs and passageways. High cliff faces shadowed with caves loom over us and there are dense island groupings, great lazy white rocks sprawled like animals just above the water. Clusters of birds, pelicans, appear to stand right on the water but are actually balancing on the tips of dangerous underwater reefs. Once I'm lost in the actual beauty of the lake, I relax a little and it isn't long before we are drawing up to the lodge dock where a young Ojibwe man named Riel—for Louis Riel, the great French-Ojibwe Métis leader who came near to establishing a Métis Nation—helps us disembark.

Kiizhikok and I settle ourselves into a cabin with a window that catches breezes off the lake. We'll hear loons laughing madly all night, sometimes close and sometimes echoing from shore to shore. Outside, the great rock we're staying on slopes dramatically into deep water. My baby actually *could* fall off this island. Still, living here will make it easy to set up our trips out to see the rock paintings. In the past, we've camped out on the islands, deciding from day to day where to pitch a tent. But I don't want to camp with baby along. She's quick, she's curious, she's smart, and she likes to put rocks in her mouth. Maybe when she's older we can deal with open fires, slippery reefs, bugs, poison ivy, and wood ticks. Well, the wood ticks we'll deal with anyway. Here's one. Here's another. They're inevitable up here. Right now, Kiizhikok appreciates a bit of grass to run across and a predictable routine.

A period of emptiness, unusual to my life, now begins, in which I can either fret or accomplish that rare thing, *the doing of nothing*. Or rather, with the baby, *the doing of what the baby wants*. This kind of doing is very much part of the trip, and although there is a dreamy blankness to it—the hours merge and the edges of the days grow fuzzy—these times when I devote my whole self to Kiizhikok are also times of great complexity and learning.

I learn, for instance, that she can keep a little stone in her mouth for an entire day. The second morning on the island I see her bend over, pick up a little white oval stone, and touch her mouth with it. But when I pry her mouth open, I can't find it. Perhaps I've just imagined that it went in. She gives me a betrayed look, clenches her jaws, and so I quit searching for the rock. We eat our breakfast and then we put on swimming suits. We sit for hours on one side of the island watching crayfish, *ashaageshiinhyag*, as they emerge in spidery shadows from the cracks of a half-submerged rock. They are fearless and dart for our toes, waving pincers. We remove them with sticks so we can ease off the rock and bob around in the lake together in our bright red life jackets.

We surprise an otter who has come to feast on the ashaageshiinhyag. He circles a cabin with a sinuous lope and then in confusion starts toward us. He pauses on the clipped grass of the island lawn. A huge glossy boy, his whiskers quiver comically as he takes our measure. With a fabulous flop he is down the rock, in the water, paddling off on his back. He watches us for a long time before he ducks under and is gone.

I'm very happy now. I wanted to see an otter on this trip because they are among my favorite animals and we know their feasting ground, just ten miles north. This place is in Seamo Bay. There, Kiizhikok's grandmother and namesake, the original Nenaa'ikiizhikok, played as a child. The otter's picnic ground is a large rock where we always find empty turtle shells. It is rather sad, but I can't help thinking how conveniently packaged a turtle is to an otter. Like a kind of Big Mac in a crushproof box. When visiting the otters' lunch spot, scattered with perfect empty shells, it is impossible not to imagine the otters lolling around sucking the turtles out and maybe munching a side of lichen or crayfish.

Late that night, as I am getting little Kiizhikok ready for bed, I see an unfamiliar flash of white and fish the stone from her mouth. I hold it in my hand and look at her in distress. My sister and brother-in-law are pediatricians. This stone is a classic choking hazard. Do you understand that, Kiizhikok? Choking hazard? I look into her warm round face and try to explain. She puts her hand on my arm in a motherly way and shakes her head indulgently. I recognize the look. My teenage daughters give it to me. *Oh, Mom, I'm fine and you just worry too much.* My head whirls. *Yes, everybody else was drunk and high on crack and heroin and many other drugs you haven't heard of don't want to and worst of all they were keeping stones in their mouths, choking hazards, while having unprotected sex, so I sat outside the party on the porch with the fireflies and thought about how I don't need to do these things to have a good time.*

I'm getting anxious about my daughters.

The fact that they are utterly responsible and I know they are safe doesn't matter. I have *got* to worry.

I'm also getting anxious about Tobasonakwut.

All of this time, Tobasonakwut is trying very hard to get to us. I always know that. I imagine that he must find a way to tow his boat to the lake, and then to dry out some spark plugs in the motor, probably. As well, he will encounter various other delays, all based on quirks of the boat and requests from other people. Besides, it is summer and that is the busiest time for Ojibwe people.

For the past two months, Tobasonakwut has been helping people meet their spirits. He does this by putting them out to fast for visions. He puts people in his sweat lodge, then into his boat, drives them out to an island, leaves them there for four days, worries and prays for and checks on them during those four days, then picks them up and feeds them ceremonially and assists them in understanding their experience. He has put out hundreds of people and picked them up hundreds of times and listened to their dreams and helped them understand their insights and their suffering. When he picks them up, as they have not eaten or drunk water during those four days, as they have heard or seen things unexpected, as they have been alone in the night and often frightened, they can barely speak. They have a certain look in their eyes. He is very careful with them.

He has been very careful with the three people, friends, who arrive the next day. I'm very glad. Now I have people to wait for him along with me. These people have fasted at the pictographs that we will visit. Every time they come to Lake of the Woods, they come prepared to become extremely hungry. This time they have decided to experience the lake in a new way—full. On the way here, however, they couldn't help stocking up on food and drink. They have developed a Pavlovian response to the lake and find it hard to believe that they will be fed. But they are fed, and copiously. The food at the fishing lodge, provided by a dedicated cook named Donna, is right out of small-town North Dakota—it is haute cuisine if you lived in Wahpeton during the mid-'70s. A relish plate. Prime rib, thick cuts of ham, tiny bowls of cauliflower drenched in cheese sauce, always some form of potato—mashed, fried, scalloped—and pitchers of iced tea. Homemade bread. Baked chicken. Pie. Salads of iceberg lettuce and pale tomato. Kiizhikok sits high on her booster seat and eats with a fork. (She's talented at this. We think it betokens an unusual and preternaturally advanced hand-eye coordination. Perhaps she'll be a famous baseball player. I won't allow her to become a fighter pilot.) Her red napkin is tucked around her neck. All around us great stuffed fish leap and gape on the walls. I feel increasingly like one of them.

Tobasonakwut arrives. During the last fifteen minutes of northern dusk light he pulls up to the dock. There he is, looming toward us with fixed weariness. I have just decided that he and the lake are one person. That is a relief. For if to describe one is also to describe the other, I am set free. Both are so vast and contradictory and full of secrets that I both despaired of and was delighted with the prospect of never getting an adequate handle on them. But now that he has actually arrived, I feel that I should introduce Tobasonakwut.

To do so, I must go back to 1688 when a twenty-year-old French explorer named Jacques de Noyon wrote about a group of people who nearly killed him when he raided their gardens of squash, corn, pumpkins, beans, and potatoes on what is now Garden Island in Lake of the Woods. According to Tobasonakwut, as de Noyon and his men approached the gardens, an arrow was fired from the woods and landed at their feet. As any rational people would, they stopped, and then from those trees there emerged a giant people, taller than any native people they'd ever met, and very frightening. He got to know them a little, and called them the People of the Cat.

Those people were Tobasonakwut's ancestors, who became the Big George family and are of the Bizhiw or Lynx dodem. Tobasonakwut's people still tend to be tall, raw-boned, rangy (handsome, I think), and with a wariness that can shift from kind to belligerent. They are not a people to be trifled with. But for all that, Tobasonakwut is exceedingly gentle. Babies seem to know this. Around my extended family, he's always the one who sits and talks to the babies. Yet he's tough in a way people who have been through too much are tough—he can sleep anywhere. Or go for days without really sleeping when his presence is required in ceremonies. Yet although he went hungry as a child, he won't eat just anything. He's finicky about his food now. He doesn't eat much meat, passes on frybread, orders salads in restaurants—unusual eating habits for an Ojibwe. As I said, he's full of contradictions, like the lake. Tobasonakwut grew up on a spit of land called Niiyaawaangashing, in a time before the Ojibwe or Anishinaabeg were removed from their homes in the islands. He is fortunate to know something of the time when his community was intact, when the bays were dotted with cabins and camps, when his extended family lived more or less by the spiritual seasons of the *Midewiwin*, the Grand Medicine teachings, and those ceremonial teachings formed the moral and social center of the community. The teachings made sense of the beauties and hardships of Ojibwe existence. He was also unfortunate, for that world was devastated in just a few years. After his people had stabilized their lives and partly recovered from the wave of nineteenth-century invasions and diseases, the Canadian government invented devastating aboriginal policies. It is his burden to have seen what survived of the Ojibwe world around him nearly demolished by death, removal, forced relocation, the poison of alcohol, and to have experienced an education that amounted to kidnapping and a brutal attempt at brainwashing.

The place where Tobasonakwut grew up, Niiyaawaangashing, is about three or four miles by water from the fishing lodge. It is very useful for us to have a base of operations so close to the places we want to visit, but it is not uncomplicated. Camp owners have become almost the only residents in land that once belonged, and by treaty rights should still belong, solely to the Ojibwe. The only native people staying at the lodge now are the fishing guides, Riel, and two other men. Tobasonakwut once worked as a fishing guide. But he knows and is part of the lake in a much more profound way than where to catch walleyes for wealthy non-Indian sport fishers. He knows the lake in a way that only indigenous people can truly know anywhere.

His people were the lake, and the lake was them. At one time, everyone who lived near the lake was essentially made of the lake. As the people lived off fish, animals, the lake's water and water plants for medicine, they were literally cell by cell composed of the lake and the lake's islands. Tobasonakwut's father once said to him, *The creator is the lake and we are the waves on the lake.* Tobasonakwut shows us the place in the heavens from which the creator descended. Their origins are familiar. The cosmology is in the surrounding landscape, in the stars, in the shapes of the rocks and islands, and in the mazinapikiniganan, the paintings that his people made on the sides of the rocks.

Niiyaawaangashing

The next day, we get into a sixteen-foot Alumacraft with a 115-horsepower motor, and we buzz out onto the lake. Before anything else, we go to visit Niiyaawaangashing. There are still two fish-camp houses standing and one tumbled-in cabin of weathered wood. Two docks twisted and upended by ice. A strong little black bear stands next to the first dock, watching us calmly. We cut the motor. The bear slides into the channel and dog-paddles with powerful assurance to the other side, where he doesn't hide himself at all, but stands up and rakes the berry bushes underneath a tree containing a huge eagle's nest. One eagle hulks stubbornly next to the nest, watching over an eaglet, whose head pops up, curious, from time to time. We skirt a long, pale boulder with a crease down the middle, just opposite the former camp, romantically secluded.

"Hundreds of Anishinaabeg were conceived on that rock," says Tobasonakwut. I look at the gray hollow in the rock—it actually looks pretty comfortable. Nobody lives at Niiyaawaangashing anymore, except the bears and eagles, and so we stop only long enough to put down tobacco. Sometimes the bears, especially the curious young, sit in the trees and watch people on the shore. Sometimes a little bear will get caught in the crotch of a tree and hang himself. When such a skeleton is found, it is very sacred to the Ojibwe and is used in religious ceremonies. Once when Tobasonakwut was little, there was a big Midewiwin or Grand Medicine lodge in the grass that is now quickly returning to scrub trees and sumac. A Midewiwin lodge is made of young bent-over popple or birch poles tied together with basswood. Spruce boughs or ferns are tied along the sides for shade. The main events of the religion are carried out in the lodge. When Tobasonakwut was about six years old, a strange event took place at the Mide lodge here at Niiyaawaangashing.

Tobasonakwut's Memory

He watched six canoes approaching from the west, one bearing a man and dog. They pulled to shore, and the explanation for their coming was given. The man with the dog had suffered an oppressive dream. It was a dream he could not mentally evade even once he woke. In the dream, he'd learned that he once had been a slave owned by the Bwaanag, the human flesh eaters, the warriors, the Sioux, who were for generations bitter enemies to the Ojibwe. As a slave, this man dreamed that he had been tied up with the dogs and, like the dogs, fed scraps, not fed at all, despised and kicked and beaten. One afternoon he just was about to die of sorrow and loneliness when it occurred to him to speak to the dog next to him, who answered. The dog told him that the dog people had been waiting for the man to talk to them. Now that he had spoken, they were willing to help him escape the Bwaanag.

There will be some feathers, said the dog, and you will chase them. When the Bwaanag look at you, they will not see a man. They will see a dog playing with some feathers. You will run after the feathers until you are far from the Bwaanag camp.

In this way, the man was freed from his degradation. The man who dreamed he was the man enslaved by the Sioux understood when he woke that he and his dog must give thanks to those dream dogs by fasting together. And so the canoes had come, accompanying him to the Midewiwin lodge, where he would fast for twelve days, his dog for four days. During those twelve days, the children were to treat the man just as the Bwaanag had, mean. Though they were to respect the dog. Tobasonakwut could not be cruel to the man, who cried and groaned in his hunger, as he lay in the lodge. The dog fasted alongside his master, and then was feasted like a human being. The man continued until he weakened so badly he could not move. But he survived, and in the end he was feasted too.

There is nothing where that lodge was but poison ivy and grass and a broken table. Tobasonakwut's dream is to rebuild the lodge there and to teach people all that he knows, including what the rock paintings mean. To this end, he has started a foundation to gather money to put up this lodge. He has also filed a claim for compensation against the Oblate Order of the Catholic Church. They were in charge of his education, but instead they stole life, innocence, and spirit from him and from his people. He thinks they should be responsible for helping to reconstruct what was lost.

Perhaps someday a Mide lodge will stand where the table has collapsed. Perhaps the old Midewiwin songs will be heard on Niiyaawaangashing once again.

Nagamonan

Songs belong to these islands. When Ojibwe people fast in these islands, the songs, even if lost for a time, always come back in dreams. The *nagamonan.* These very old songs are as old as the rock paintings. Songs were composed, often by those who owned drums, for honor, for celebration, for beauty, for love. There is one particular song that haunts Tobasonakwut and has, as well, a special meaning for me. Our friends often sing this song in their sweat lodge. It is a song used to help those struggling with the pitiless, uncanny, and baffling disease that is alcoholism. The words of the song, *Kiiwashkwe biishki indigo anishaa dash indigo,* are the words of a long-ago drunk who found his way to sobriety not through a twelve-step program, but through the intervention of a powerful spirit. All of this happened during the eighteenth century, when the fur trade began the first wave of alterations that would forever shift the economic, social, and spiritual balance of Ojibwe life in Lake of the Woods.

Tobasonakwut always begins his story of this song by attributing it to his uncle Kwekwekibiness. Very traditional people are very careful about attribution. When a story begins there is a prefacing history of that story's origin that is as complicated as the Modern Language Association guidelines to form in footnotes.

In this story, there was a young man, an extraordinary hunter, known as unusually strong and of a generous nature. He began to sell his furs to the first trader in the islands. At first, the young hunter acquired blankets, fire strikers, kettles, guns, and ammunition. He traded for things he needed, his family needed, his wife, his children. But eventually, he traded for liquor too.

A form of trader's rum, mixed with hot pepper and tobacco, became his pleasure. He bought a little more each time he came with piles of beaver skins. The trader began to provide him with the liquor before they finished their negotiations, and soon the young man woke from long binges and found that he owed the trader, that he had drunk up his pay and then some. At last, he began trading for the rum alone. His children left him, his wife left him, his whole family stayed away from him. The animals stayed away from him too. It was no use hunting, so he traded his gun for a keg. It was no use trapping, so he drank away his traps. Finally, it was no use begging either. No use in anything. The trader's liquor had eaten his life, his loves, his strength, his mind, his will, and all but a fraction of his spirit.

This tiny part of his spirit, this fraction of the man that was still a man, decided that it would disappear into the wilderness. So the young man walked away from the trading house and from all of the trade goods including the rum. He walked off into the snow without a blanket and without a gun. He walked until he was blinded by the snow glare, exhausted to the last degree. In the deepest moment of despair he'd ever known, he threw himself down in a trackless place, at the mercy of the spirits. While he was face down in the snow, and as he determined that he surely would die, he heard a song.

The nagamon began like this, Kiiwashkwe biishki indigo anishaa dash indigo. I am a drunk. I am nothing. The song went on and he sang the whole of it into the place beyond the bottom of a drinking cup that is the darkest place on Earth. As he sang this song, over and over, and as he waited to die, this young man heard a voice.

It was the voice of the Kwiingwa'aage.

The Kwiingwa'aage is a spirit of dark strength and cleverness represented by an animal, the wolverine. Among the Ojibwe, this animal has an almost supernatural reputation. There is one who steals from your traps and cannot be caught. There is one who you know is watching you, but you cannot see him or hear him. There is an animal who follows you just out of sight. It is deathless, lonely, and somewhat strange in his contempt for human intelligence. He easily outwits the smartest hunters.

When the creator passed near the Earth in the form of a tailed light, that was the Kwiingwa'aage. When a man feels eyes at his back and experiences a thrill of unreasonable fear out in the woods, that is the Kwiingwa'aage. Perhaps because he is so fearless, so impervious to pain, so dangerously strong, the spirit of the Kwiingwa'aage is the only one that can address the problems of the *schkwebii*, the alcoholic. For the disease is without pity just as is the animal. Alcohol is cunning, and it is phenomenally deceptive. So when the animal spoke to the young man, and said that he had been watching him, and that he had given this young man a song, it might have been the first time the Kwiingwa'aage was known to pity anyone.

And if it was the first time that this spirit had showed pity, in all the years of Ojibwe hardship, then it goes to show how terrible this scourge of alcohol was, and how low it laid the people.

The voice of the Kwiingwa'aage saved the young man though, and he got rid of the trader's poison and recovered his life.

There are no Anishinaabeg, including mixed-bloods like me, whose lives have not been affected by the perplexing pains of addiction. The degraded longing and despair of alcoholism changes even the most intelligent among us. And so when we regard the place where the song given by the Kwiingwa'aage was first heard by the young man so long ago, it is for me a personal moment. I hold our baby tighter and we put out handfuls of tobacco.

The Four Stones

Tobasonakwut's copy of the big book of Alcoholics Anonymous is covered with a handmade leather case. It is marked and thumbed, interleaved with personal notes and ribbons. It is like a preacher's bible, or a writer's favorite dictionary. He has carried the twelve steps with him for over thirty-five years, but his uncle, Kwekwekibiness, who knew nothing of the steps, surprised him once by telling him something about the book that he had not perceived.

Kwekwekibiness was devoted to the sweat lodge ceremony, in which stones are super heated and then cooled with water to produce a healing steam. In every Ojibwe ceremony, the number four is sacred—four seasons, four directions, four phases of life, four of everything. Kwekwekibiness held Tobasonakwut's book and told him that it contained four stones. Intrigued, Tobasonakwut examined the book for the stones and after reading it painstakingly found three. He couldn't find the last until one day he noticed, in the beginning of the book, a gravestone.

John Tanner and the Landscape of Hunger

This is John Tanner country—where he was always hungry. One of my favorite books, *The Falcon, a Narrative of the Captivity and Adventures of John Tanner During Thirty Years Residence among the Indians in the Interior of North America,* is about the relentless efforts of a man to feed himself. My sisters and I read this book in its old Ross and Haines edition until the spine gave, the pages tumbled out and were held together with a rubber band. John Tanner's narrative exerted a fascination on us, and not only because one of our ancestors was mentioned in its pages, but because of the enigma of John Tanner himself. My sister Lise says that it is the only true sequel to that great American novel, *The Adventures of Huckleberry Finn,* which ends when Huck and Jim light out for the territory. On the first page of his narrative John Tanner wishes, as a boy, that he could go and live with the Indians. During the next few pages he is, indeed, captured by the Shawnee. It is 1789, and the rest of the novel is about what exactly happens in the "territory."

John Tanner was brought north, sold, adopted, and from then on lived entirely as an Ojibwe. For the most part, he hunted throughout Lake of the Woods country and into Rainy Lake, the exact range of the area I'm visiting on this trip. I've read his narrative so often that it is a constant mental reference. I see this region as it is and was. When I think about John Tanner's life the flimsy billboards, border crossings, cheap plastic gas station signs, and hopeful fishing lodge ads look pathetically superimposed on a region harsh, mystical, quite beyond the practical efforts of human beings to tame it. Out here on the lake, those human efforts are sparse and seasonal. It doesn't take much imagination to see myself in Tanner's world.

John Tanner led a feast or famine life. His tale was told after he had attempted to return to civilization and found its restrictions irksome. Tanner, whose Indian name was Shaw-shaw-wa-Be-na-se, or Falcon, was captured at nine years old, specifically to comfort a woman who'd lost her own son. But his stepfather and brother nearly killed him and he was fortunate enough to be sold to an extraordinary and resourceful Ojibwe woman, Net-no-kwa, whom he came to love. His portrait of Net-no-kwa is a treasure. Tanner had a gift for description and an ear for anecdote, and in his voice Net-no-kwa is a stereotype-busting powermonger. When she approached the fort at Mackinac with her flag flying from her boat (it was probably a flag that described her personal dream vision), she was saluted by the fort's gun. She was a shrewd trader, an observant hunter, and a medicine woman who also got smashed on whiskey from time to time. She saved her family many times with her resourcefulness in times of crisis, and she and Tanner developed a particular affection for one another. "Though Net-no-kwa was now decrepit and infirm," he says near the end of her life, "I felt the strongest regard for her and continued to do so while she lived."

Tanner had a clear eye and in his narrative he provides detailed descriptions of the world around him. A terrified female bear picks up her cub and cradles it like a human. He recounts his surprise at a porcupine's trusting stupidity and notes that it was quite tasty. An otter exhausts him with its tenacious fury when he tries to kill it with his bare hands. Tanner attended to animal behavior with a terrible fixity of purpose, for game was the only real food and his relationship with nature was one of practical survival.

At the leanest times, Tanner's family was forced to boil and eat their own moccasins, to subsist on the inner bark of trees or dead vines. During the best of times, the food was eaten all at once and drink, if there was any, consumed until it disappeared. Indeed, the kind of life where a few people killed a fat moose and polished it entirely off in a few days is mirrored in the binge or abstinence style of drinking that Tanner describes. Not a life for the moderate. Not a life for the faint of heart. Tanner's ordinary feats of hunting endurance are almost beyond comprehension in these days of radio-collared bear dogs and high-powered telescopic rifles. And yet he was by his own account no more than a mediocre hunter, who was patiently instructed by Ojibwe who had survived for millennia without guns or steel:

> I had occasion to go to the trading house on Red River, and I started in company with a half-breed ... who was mounted on a fleet horse. The distance we had to travel has since been called, by the English settlers, seventy miles. We rode and went on foot by turns, and the one who was on foot kept hold of the horse's tail and ran. We passed over the whole distance in one day.

When I returned to my family I had
but seven bullets left, but as there was
no trader near, I could not at present get
more. With those seven I killed twenty
moose and elk. Often times, in shooting a
moose or elk, the ball does not pass entirely
through and can be used again.

Visiting his family in Kentucky after having lived
virtually all of his life in the north woods, John Tanner fell
ill. He grew claustrophobic when nursed inside of a house,
and had to sleep outside in his brother's yard to restore his
strength. Once he returned to Sault Ste. Marie and told his
story, he vanished. He was suspected of a murder but that
charge was later thought false. He never turned up. As Lise
says, "He vanished into his own legend." His end was as
mysterious and tragic as the outline of his life in this beautiful, unforgiving country. As he was to all respects a
"white Indian," and saw the world as an Ojibwe, his is the
first narrative of native life from an Ojibwe point of view.

CHAPTER THREE

Rock Paintings

More About Age

One of the first questions people ask about the rock paintings is how old they are—complicated answer. There is no completely accurate way to date rock paintings. Some are hundreds of years old, and others thousands of years. The Anishinaabe have been in Lake of the Woods forever, according to Tobasonakwut. Since at least two thousand years before the birth of Christ, according to archaeologists. One thing certain is that the paintings were made by the ancestors of the present-day Anishinaabeg, for the ancient symbols on the rocks are as familiar and recognizable to Tobasonakwut as are, say, highway and airport and deer crossing signs to contemporary Americans. Of course, the rock paintings are not just pointer signs. They hold far more significance. They refer to a spiritual geography, and are meant to provide teaching and dream guides to generations of Anishinaabeg.

Akawe Asema

The rock paintings are alive. This is more important than anything else that I can say about them. As if to prove this point, we see as we approach Painted Rock Island that a boat has paused. It is a silver fishing boat with a medium horsepower outboard motor. A man leans over and scoops a handful of tobacco from a pouch, places it before the painting, and then maneuvers his boat out and goes on. *Akawe asema.* First offer tobacco. This makes Tobasonakwut extremely happy, as do all the offerings that we will see as we visit the other paintings. It is evidence to him that the spiritual life of his people is in the process of recovery. He swerves the boat out and chases down the man who made the offering, and then, seeing who he is, waves and cuts away. He is doubly pleased because he knows where this man sets his nets, and knows that he went ten or twelve miles out of his way to visit the rock painting. It is sunset now and will be dark before the man returns to his dock.

The Wild Rice Spirit

The long rays of the deepening sun reach through the channel. As we draw our boat up to the rock painting, the light warms the face of what was once a cliff. I am standing before the rock wall of Painted Rock Island and trying to read it like a book. I don't know the language, though. The painting spreads across a ten- or twelve-foot rectangle of smooth rock, and includes several spirit figures as well as diagrams of teachings. The deep light pulls the figures from the rock. They seem to glow from the inside, a vibrant golden red. For a long while, I am only interested in the visual experience of standing at eye level with the central figures in the rock. They are simple and extremely powerful. One is a horned human figure and the other a stylized spirit figure who Tobasonakwut calls, lovingly, the *Manoominikeshii,* or the wild rice spirit.

Once you know what it is, the wild rice spirit looks exactly like itself. A spiritualized wild rice plant. Beautifully drawn, economically imagined. I have no doubt that this figure appeared to the painter in a dream, for I have had such dreams, and I have heard such dreams described. The spirits of things have a certain look to them, a family resemblance. This particular spirit of the wild rice crop is invoked and fussed over, worried over, just as the plants are checked throughout the summer for signs of ripening.

This year, on Lake of the Woods, the rice looks dismal. Because the high waters have invaded a whole new level of recently established rice beds, the rice is leggy and will flop over before it can be harvested. Earlier in the day, we stopped to examine Tobasonakwut's family rice beds. At this time of the year, mid-July, the rice is especially beautiful. It is in the floating leaf stage and makes a pattern on the water like bright green floating hair. *Kiimaagoogan,* it is called. But upon pulling up a stalk Tobasonakwut says sadly, "There's nothing in this loonshit," meaning he cannot find the seed in the roots. All the energy of the plant has gone into growing itself high enough to survive the depth of the water. There will not be enough reserve strength left in the plant to produce a harvest. "And then," Tobasonakwut goes on, "if your parents had no children, you can't have children." In other words, the rice crop will be affected for years.

So perhaps this year it is especially important to ask for some help from the Manoominikeshii.

When the pictures were painted, the lake was a full nine feet lower, and as it is nearly four feet higher this year than usual, some paintings of course are submerged. The water level is a political as well as natural process—it is in most large lakes now. From the beginning, that the provincial government allowed the lake levels to rise infuriated the Anishinaabeg, as the water ruined thousands of acres of wild rice beds. As it is, I mentally add about one story of rock to the painting, which at present lies only a few feet out of the water.

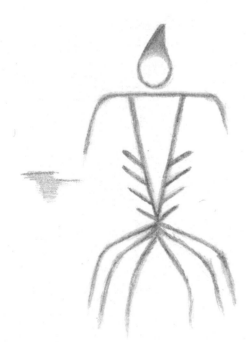

This is a feminine-looking drawing. The language of the wild rice harvest is intensely erotic and often comically sexualized. If the stalk is floppy, it is a poor erection. Too wet, it is a penis soaking in its favorite place. Half hard, full, hairy, the metaphors go on and on. Everything is sexual, the way of the world is to be sexual, and it is good (although often ridiculous). The great teacher of the Anishinaabeg, whose intellectual prints are also on this rock, was a being called Nanabozho, or Winabojo. He was wise, he was clever, he was a sexual idiot, a glutton, full of miscalculations and bravado. He gave medicines to the Ojibwe, one of the primary being laughter.

The Horned Man

This is the figure that glows brightest from the rock. He is not a devil, and he isn't throwing away a Christian cross—the local white Christian interpretation of the painting, which has led to its close call at defacement. (At the figure's far right, in white paint, I can still make out

Jesus Christ in fairly neat lettering. But the thirty-year-old graffiti has nearly flaked off, while the original painted figures still blaze true.) As I stand before the painting, I come to believe that the horned figure is a self-portrait of the artist.

Books. Why? So we can talk to you even though we are dead. Here we are, the writer and I, regarding each other.

Horns connote intellectual and spiritual activity— important to us both and used on many of the rock paintings all across the Canadian Shield. The cross that the figure is holding over the rectangular water drum probably signifies the degree that the painter had reached in the hierarchy of knowledge that composes the formal structure of the Ojibwe religion, the Midewiwin. The cross is the sign of the fourth degree, and as well, there are four Mide squares stacked at the figure's left-hand side, again revealing the position of the painter in the Mide lodge.

I quickly grow fond of this squat, rosy, hieratic figure. His stance is both proud and somewhat comical, the bent legs strong and stocky. His arms are raised but he doesn't seem to be praying as much as dancing, ready to spring into the air, off the rock. When this rock was painted on a cliff, the water below was not a channel but a small lake that probably flooded periodically, allowing fish to exit and enter. Perhaps it was a camping or a teaching place, or possibly even a productive wild rice bed. Very likely it was a place where the Mide lodge was built, like Niiyaawaangashing. The painter may have been a Mide teacher, eager to leave instructions and to tell people about the activities that took place here.

Most of the major forms of communication with the spirit world are visible in this painting—the Mide lodge, the sweat lodge or *madoodiswan,* the shake tent. The horned figure beats a water drum. Such drums are extremely resonant, and their tone changes beautifully according to the level of the water and the player's skill at shifting the water in the drum while beating it. (Anyone curious about the sound of the water drum can buy a CD and listen to the winners of a recent Native American Grammy, the singers Verdell Primeaux and Johnny Mike, *Bless The People*.) The water drum is a healing drum. In the pictograph a bear floats over the drum, and a line between the horned figure and the bear connects them with the sky world.

The line is a sign of power and communication. It is sound, speech, song. The lines drawn between things in Ojibwe pictographs are extremely important, for they express relationships, usually between a human and a supernatural being. Wavy lines are most impressive, for they signify direct visionary information, talk from spirit to spirit. In the work of some contemporary Ojibwe artists, Joe Geshick, Blake Debassige, and of course Norval Morrisseau, the line is still used to signify spiritual inter-action. Contemporary native art is not just influenced by the conventions invented by the rock painters, it is a continuation, evidence of the vitality of Ojibwe art.

The Bay of Baby Spirits

Looking on a map at the little bay we are going to travel, my friend, who is in training as a *doulah* or birth assistant, says no wonder it is known as the home of baby spirits— the bay is thin and winding and looks like a fallopian tube. The bay of little spirits is a courting bay, the water shallow and romantic. To either side, the rich young undergrowth is said to be inhabited by the spirits of babies who choose humans, as they pass, to come and live with. Traveling slowly down the shallow channel, I stroke the tender spot upon Kiizhikok's head, the fontanel, which has nearly shut. I've heard it said that until it does the baby still hears spirits talking. If they're out there, if they're talking to her, I hope they are warning her that it is dangerous to hide stones in her mouth.

Suddenly we come upon three young moose, gangly and playful. Instead of climbing onto land, one clomps into the water and then swims along beside us. Her long rabbity ears cock toward us from time to time, and she doesn't seem particularly frightened. Her Joe Camel nose held high, she rolls her eyes at us. Those odd Twiggy legs and knobby knees work smoothly, powerfully. A wonderful swimmer, she at last veers away into the reeds and cattails. I am very surprised that this happened. According to John Tanner the wary moose is the most difficult of animals to hunt. But then, these are very young moose and our baby is in the boat. I harbor the irrational notion that animals are curious about Kiizhikok and show themselves around her, that her presence is a kind of magnet to them. And it is true, not only do we see animals but they seem unafraid of her, like the otter, like the moose, and the constantly wheeling eagles and pelicans. The animals come close as if they want to get a good look at this child whose ancestors watched their ancestors, whose grandmother ate their grandmothers, whose father was stolen from among them by priests.

Mirage Islands

When the water is high like it is this year, large pieces of bog pull free of the lake bottom and drift all through the bays and channels. You fall asleep looking at a certain shoreline, memorizing the sweep of it, and by morning the shape has shifted and the bog has moved on. When these bogs attach to islands, they can change its shape instantly, but often they merely bounce against the island until they fall apart. Lodge owners get their guide boats out and push the bogs into the lake currents. Close up, rising out of deep water, they are deceptively solid looking. They are a rich biomass composed of reeds, young willow, *wiikenh,* cattails.

Cattails are a useful plant whose roots are edible, whose tails when puffed out are a perfect diapering material for the tender new bottoms of Anishinaabeg babies, used to stuff in the bags of cradleboards. Reeds were used for floor covering, woven into mats. Wiikenh, or sweet-flag, is the star of the floating bog, though, a medicine with every possible use. "Where there is wiikenh, there are Anishinaabeg," says Tobasonakwut. Wiikenh is the ultimate medicine. He investigates each floating bog, hoping to pick it easily, for when rooted it is difficult to wrench from the mud.

Looking at these bogs it is easy to see how, once, when a raiding party of Bwaanag had camped in Ojibwe country, they were driven out by use of a floating bog. The warriors entered the bog from underneath and swam it to the shore of the Bwaanag camp, like Birnam Wood come to Dunsinane. From that bog, they attacked and drove the Bwaanag out.

Massacre Island

It is not considered wise to point a finger at any island, especially this one. The Ojibwe use mouth or head to indicate direction, and are often humorously mocked for "pointing with the lips." But it is impolite to point a finger at people, and the islands as well. Pointing at the islands is like challenging them. And you don't want to challenge anything this powerful.

Massacre Island is a forbidden place. Recently, two men who tried to fast there were bothered the entire night by ghosts. As we approach the island, I feel its brooding presence. I can't tell whether this island is a formidable place because of its history, or whether it possesses a somber gravity all on its own. But the very look of the place disturbs me. Massacre Island is located where the lake deepens. Sounds travel farther, the air thins, the waves go flat. Its rocks sloping down to the water are not the pale pink flecked granite of the other islands, but a heavy gray nearly black in places and streaked with a fierce red-gold lichen.

On this island, the Ojibwe wiped out an entire party of Sioux, or Bwaanag. As Tobasonakwut tells it, the entire island was ringed by Ojibwe canoes. At a signal, the *sasawkwe,* the war whoop, a terrifying and a bloodthirsty shrill, was raised. From one canoe to the next, it traveled, a ring of horrifying sound. The canoes advanced four times. The sasawkwe was raised four times. On the last time, the Ojibwe paddlers surged all the way forward, beached their canoes, and stormed the Bwaanag. He shows where the warriors died, including one who staked himself into the earth and fought all comers who entered his circle, until he was overwhelmed.

Atisikan

The paint, *atisikan,* should be patented, says Tobasonakwut. It is an eternal paint. The Ojibwe Sharpee paint. It works on anything. When he was little he often watched the paint being prepared. It was used for other things, besides painting on rocks. For burial, for bringing people into the religion, for teachings, for decorating request sticks and Mide stakes.

The recipes for paints used by other tribes are often based on vermillion from outcroppings of cinnabar. The Inuit used blood and charcoal. Burnt plum seeds and bull rushes were mixed into a black paint by the Klamath, and many tribes used blue carbonate of copper. Later, as we walk the Kaawiikwethawangag, the Eternal Sands, I will find some of the mysterious ingredients of the Ojibwe atisikan at my feet, then jumping from the lake.

Obabikon

On a great gray sweep of boulder, high above Obabikon channel, a rock painting gives instructions to the spirit on how to travel from this life into the next life. Such a journey takes four days and is filled with difficulties.

For that reason, loved ones provide the spirit with food, spirit dishes, and encouragement in the form of prayers and songs. We climb to the painting with tobacco and leave handfuls by the first painting, a line with four straight, sweeping branches, and the second painting, which is of a *mikinaak,* or turtle.

The mikinaak has immense significance in Ojibwe life. As there are thirteen plates in its back, it is associated with the thirteen moons in the yearly cycle, and also with women. It was women, says Tobasonakwut, who were responsible for beginning Ojibwe mathematical calculations. They began because they had to be concerned with their own cycles, had to count the days so that they would know when they would be fertile. They had to keep close track of the moon, and had to relate it to their bodies in order to predict the births of their children. And they had to be accurate, so that they could adequately prepare. In a harsh Ojibwe winter, giving birth in an unprotected spot could be lethal. Women had to prepare to be near relatives and other knowledgeable women. Mathematics wasn't abstract. It was intimate. Dividing and multiplying and factoring were concerns of the body, and of survival.

Whitefish Bay

To get into Whitefish Bay from where we are will require lots of sandwiches, water, a full gas tank, and two extra five-gallon plastic gas containers that ride in front when full. We start early on a tremendously hot morning. By now, I'm much happier in a boat. I still have the usual fantasy, on starting out, involving the rock and the swim to shore towing Kiizhikok, but by now I'm used to it. I try to move on quickly and enjoy the breeze whipping with heroic freshness off the lake. Whitefish Bay connects to Lake of the Woods via a peculiar contraption called a boat trolley. This is a suspicious-looking, wood-ribbed basket that the boat is floated onto. By sheer muscle power, turning a big red metal wheel that moves the trolley basket along a set of metal tracks, the boat is painfully transferred. Once on the other side of the concrete channel, we reload ourselves and start off, into Whitefish Bay.

First, we pause at the place where Tobasonakwut was born, a quiet little bay of old-growth pine and soft duff. Just after he and his brother were born, Tobasonakwut's name was discovered by his father, who gazed out into the bay and saw a certain type of cloud cover, low and even. Tobasonakwut. His twin was named for a small bird that visited his mother shortly after the birth. She has told Tobasonakwut that as this is the type of bird who nests in the same place year after year, if he ever sees one on a visit it will be a relative of the one who named his brother.

As he is sitting beneath a tree that must have been a sapling when he was born, as he is singing to his daughter, I realize that after thousands of years of continual habitation and birth on the shores of this lake, Tobasonakwut is one of the last human beings who will ever be born out on these islands.

Wiikenh

Wiikenh tea strengthens the immune system. Mixed with a mashed waterlily root, *okundamoh,* it draws out infection and poison. Speakers chew wiikenh to keep their throats clear, and singers chew it to strengthen their voices at the drum. As we enter a long channel filled with shallow water and small flooded bays, Tobasonakwut sees vast clumps of bright green-gold reeds and mutters, over and over, "So much wiikenh!" This is not the gloating sound I've heard before in his voice when discovering so much medicine. Rather, he is distressed that it should be sprouting in such tremendous abundance and no one else has come to pick it. His tone implies that this should all have been harvested, that the endless thick fringe of plants along the shores is an almost painful sight. One thing is sure, he can't pass it up, and for about an hour we putter along, stopping from time to time for him to lean over the prow of the boat and pull up the long tough bundles of muddy roots. He slices them off with a very sharp hunting knife while I sit behind the wheel of the boat with the baby.

Wiikenh gathering is very boring to her, but she has decided to be lulled into a state of contemplation by a combination of breast milk and boat engine. Indeed, every time she gets into the boat now, she tips her head dreamily toward my nipple. I've grown used to having her there. I've filmed eagles and those young moose, dancing loons and *zhegeg,* pelicans, with one hand while she nurses away. Indeed, though I haven't mentioned it, I have been filming everything I've described all along, as well as somehow brandishing a pen and notebook, all while nursing. One grows used to it.

Sometimes I look at men, at the way most of them move so freely in the world, without a baby attached, and it seems to me very strange. Sometimes it is enviable. Mostly, it is not. For at night, as she curls up or sprawls next to me and as I fall asleep, I hold onto her foot. This is as much for my comfort as to make sure that she doesn't fall off the bed. As I'm drifting away, I feel sorry for anyone else who is not falling asleep this way, holding onto her baby's foot. The world is calm and clear. I wish for nothing. I am not nervous about the future. Her toes curl around my fingers. I could even stop writing books.

Spirit Bay

The name on the map is actually Devil's Bay, so tiresome and so insulting. Squaw Rock. Devil's This and Devil's That. Indian or Tomahawk Anything. There's no use railing. You know it as well as I do. Some day, when there is nothing more important to do, the Anishinaabeg will demand that all the names be changed. For it was obviously the rock painting at the entrance to the bay that inspired the name. It is not a devil, of course, but a spirit in communication with the unknowable. Another horned figure, only this time enormous, imposing, and much older than the one in Lake of the Woods.

This spirit figure, horns pointed, wavering, and with arms upraised, is fading to a yellow-gold stain in the rock. It is a huge figure, looming all the way up the nine- or ten-foot flat of the stone. At the base of this painting, there is a small ledge. Upon it, a white polo shirt has been carefully folded, an offering, as well as a pair of jeans. The offerings are made out of respect, for personal reasons, or to ask the spirit of the painting for help. There are three rolls of cloth, tied with ribbons. Asema. Again, here are the offerings, the signs that the rock paintings are alive and still respected by the Anishinaabeg.

Binessi

I get very excited when I see the thunderbird pictured on a cliff far above the water. It is so beautifully painted, so fluid and powerful even glimpsed from forty feet below. "Are you strong? Are you agile?" Tobasonakwut asks. "If you are you should climb up to that rock. You'll never be sorry that you did." I believe him. I grab my camera, my tobacco offering, and retie my running shoes. I already have my twenty extra pounds left over from having a baby. I am just pretending that I am strong and agile. Really, I'm soft and clumsy, but I want to see the painting. I am on fire to see it. I want to stand before that painting because I know that it is one of the most beautiful paintings I will have ever seen. Put up there out of reach or within difficult reach for that very reason. At that moment, I just want to see it because it is beautiful, not because I'll get some spiritual gift.

The climb is hard, though of course it looked easy from below. Like all women are accused of doing, I claw my way to the top. Sweaty, heart pounding, I finally know I'm there. All I have to do is inch forward and step around the edge of the cliff, but that's the thing. I have to step around one particular rock and it looks like there's nothing below it or on the other side. I could fall into the rocks. My children could be left motherless. Or I could simply get hurt, which is not simple at all. I calculate. The nearest hospital is hours away and there is that trolley contraption. So I don't go around the rock, but seek another route. I continue climbing until I'm over the top of the cliff. Still, I can't see down. I don't know how to get down to the paintings. Again, I nearly take the chance and lower myself over the cliff but I can't see how far I'd fall. Finally, looking far, far down at my baby in her tiny life jacket, I know I'm a mother and I just can't do it.

Climbing back into the boat is admitting defeat.

"Give me the camera, and tobacco," says Tobasonakwut.

"No!" I say. "Don't do it!"

"Why? If you can't make it then you'll feel bad if I do?"

"Just like a guy, so competitive! Because you *will* go around the corner of that rock and you'll fall and kill yourself."

"I will not fall. I've done this before."

"How many years ago?"

"A few."

With terse dignity, Tobasonakwut goes. He's an incredible climber and regularly shames the twenty-somethings who come to fast on the rock cliffs by climbing past them and even dragging up their gear. I know he'll make it. He'll do something ridiculous, maybe even get hurt, but he'll manage to get right next to the paintings.

He's always poking around in the islands. Once, he described a rockslide he started coming down from a cliff like this one. Remembering this, I maneuver the boat away from a skid of rocks on the south side of the cliff, though he didn't go up that route. Anyway, he had a ter-rifying ski down on the boulders and at the bottom one bounced high in the air, over him, and its point landed right between the first and second toe of his right foot. He said that he'd done something mildly offensive to the rocks. He'd thrown one down to see what happened. That's how the landslide started. When the boulder bounced down on his foot, he thought it would slice his foot off. But when he looked down his foot was still there.

Just a crushed place between his toes. It was as if, he said, the rocks, the grandfathers had said, "Don't fool around with us."

And now he's climbing rocks again.

It's no use. The best I can do is make sure that the baby's comfortable. I might as well be comfortable too. I take a fat little peanut butter sandwich from the cooler and munch dreamily, while nursing, and after a while the wind in the pines and the chatter of birds lull us into a peaceful torpor. I forget to watch for him, forget the all important ascent. From somewhere, at some point, I hear him call but he doesn't sound in distress so I just let my mind float out onto the lake.

Then he's back.

"Did you see me up there?"

"No!" I feel guilty, awful. Here he is about as old as I'll be when Kiizhikok graduates from high school and I didn't take the trouble to film him as he made the dangerous climb to the rock paintings. He hands over the camera. Ashamed of my distracted laziness, I put it away.

"How did you do it?" I ask quietly.

"Oh, jumped."

"What?"

"Jumped."

I'm immediately just a little pissed off. "You jumped? You could have broken your leg!"

"It was only six feet."

"More like fifteen feet."

"Well, if you hang down, it comes to ..."

"Don't ever do that again!"

We travel for a while, heading back for the boat trolley, and I brood on his unlikely stubborn-headed insistence that he's still a young man. How long will it take before he really hurts himself? He's scarred and burnt. Just last winter a red hot stone from a sweat lodge brushed up against his calf and left a deep hole. His back and chest are pitted with sun-dance scars and one of his eyebrows was smashed sideways in a boxing match. He took so many punches to the head while a boxer that he has to take special eyedrops now to relieve the pressure on his optic nerve.

"You've got to quit doing things like this," I say softly, but I know I will have no effect, and besides, this is one of the reasons I love him. He's a little crazy, in a good way, half teenager and half *akiwenzii.*

He doesn't answer, just keeps steering the boat, munching trail mix.

When we get to the boat trolley I am further convinced that animals love the baby because it happens again. This time it is a nice fat *waboose,* a grown rabbit. The rabbit sees us from across the shallow boat channel and behaves just like a friendly little dog. It hops down onto the trolley mechanism while Tobasonakwut is laboriously turning the wheel. The little rabbit crosses the water using a rail as a bridge, and comes curiously up to me. The rabbit looks right at the baby. Just as when the otter came toward us, I'm a bit unnerved. I suddenly imagine that this rabbit will bounce charmingly close, and then bare vampire teeth. But it merely inspects us, turns, and hops away calmly.

All right, I think, animals *do* love the baby.

Now that we're over the channel and into Lake of the Woods again, I try hard to let go of my agitation about Tobasonakwut's dangerous rock climb. We start talking about the thunderbird pictured in the rock painting that I didn't get to. I did take a movie picture of it and

Tobasonakwut surely snapped some up-close shots, I think, consoling myself. That thunderbird is very graceful, and there is a handprint with it. It is still the most beautiful bird I have ever seen.

Binessiwag

These spirits are particular about what they're called—they prefer *Binessiwag* to *Animikiig.* They're very powerful. Thunder is the beating of their wings. Lightning flashes from their eyes. You don't want to rile the young ones, as they are the most unpredictable. When a storm approaches, traditional Ojibwe cover all the shiny objects—mirror and cooking pans—so as not to attract the attention of the Binessiwag. A feather over the door lets them know Anishinaabeg are at home. They will avoid that house. It is important, when the Binessiwag appear, at any time of the day or night, to offer tobacco.

The only natural enemy of these immensely strong beings are the great snakes, the *Ginebigoog,* who live underwater. These snakes are said to travel from lake to lake via an underground network of watery tunnels that lies beneath northern Minnesota and Ontario. There is an ongoing feud between these two powerful supernatural beings. The young Binessiwag, those that come out in spring, are the most volatile, the most unpredictable.

Anyone who has experienced a violent spring thunderstorm in the north woods can attest to this truth. As we have perfect weather, we don't need to appease the Binessiwag. Day after day the morning sun shines clear. The Earth heats up. The water gleams like metal. The sky by noon is a hot deep blue.

The Eternal Sands

Kaawiikwethawangag, they are called, the Eternal Sands. John Tanner must have approached from the south, for he said, that "this lake is called by the Indians Pub-be-kwaw-waung-gaw Sau-gi-e-gun, 'the Lake of the Sand Hills.' Why it is called 'Lake of the Woods' by the whites, I cannot tell, as there is not much wood about it." And it is true, the lake is very different in character when approached from this direction. Gorgeous and deserted sand beaches stretch around the southeast side of Big Island, the reserve that Tobasonakwut's mother, the original Nenaa'ikiizhikok, came from. The great island is now empty of people, the villages abandoned since shortly after World War II.

Even though Canada's aboriginal people could not vote and were being forced from their lands and educated by force, they fought in both World Wars. One of Tobasonakwut's uncles, a soldier, came home to Big Island much affected by the fighting. He was silent, withdrawn, and stayed away from his family. Then his little son, a small boy named Wabijiis, came down with an unusual fever.

Such was the terror of disease, at the time, that it was decided that once the boy died the village would break up and the people disperse to Seamo Bay and Niiyaawaangashing. The little boy's grave was dug with paddles—the people wanted to bury him the old way and not use metal. A prayer flag was erected near. The little boy Wabijiis was the last person buried on Big Island, and his grave and all that remains of the village is now grown over with young trees.

Nameh

All of a sudden between our boat and the fringed woods a great fish vaults up into the air. I've seen muskies. I walk around a Minneapolis lake of which signs warn MUSKELUNGE ARE IN THESE WATERS. Once, I saw an Uptown Minneapolis type, dressed in tight black jeans and tight black T, wearing a suit jacket, fishing in a very cool way. Cool until he hooked a vast muskie. His screams echoed along the sedate bike paths and the fish he dragged forth was soon surrounded by Rollerbladers, joggers, and awestruck pink- and blue-haired teens. The fish I just saw was not a muskie. It was even bigger. Tobasonakwut sees it from the corner of his eye and slows the boat down.

"Asema," he says, and puts the tobacco in the water. That fish was the *nameh*. The sturgeon. Tobasonakwut is happy and moved to see it because, he says, "They rarely show themselves like that."

Once again, I'm sure it is the baby. The sturgeon seemed to take flight above the water, rising in a pale thrust and falling on its back. The sturgeon is a living relic of life before the age of the dinosaurs, and to see one is to obtain a glimpse of life 200 million years ago. I've never seen one of these fish in the wild before, much less grown large. I've only seen tiny, fish hatchery, Pallid Sturgeon that a relative of mine who works for the North Dakota Department of Natural Resources was raising to stock the Missouri River. Nameh, *Acipenser fulvescens Rafinesque,* the Lake Sturgeon, is long-lived and can grow to more than eight feet. The Lake of the Woods record fish was a lake sturgeon weighing 238 pounds. Tobasonakwut says they can grow over twice that large. Males live into their forties. Female sturgeon can live over one hundred years, but they only spawn every four years, and not until they are in their twenties.

The sturgeon up here on Lake of the Woods were the buffalo of the Ojibwe. Greed and overfishing by non-Indians caused their population to crash around the turn of the nineteenth century, when, along with the Great Lakes, Lake of the Woods became one of the world's principal suppliers of caviar. The sturgeon were indiscriminately taken by the non-Indian fisheries for their roe, much as the buffalo hunters took only the buffalo tongues. They were stacked like cordwood all along the lake and often left to rot. An agonizing sight for the Ojibwe, who revere the sturgeon and who knew its secrets.

Long before fish-farming, the Ojibwe had traditional "sturgeon gardens," shallow and protected parts of the lake where they mixed eggs and sperm and protected the baby sturgeon from predators. The eggs and sperm were mixed together with an eagle feather in an act both sacred and ordinary. These days, the Ontario Ministry of Natural Resources and tribal communities raise sturgeon.

A conservation program begun ninety-nine years ago, in Lake Winnebago near Shawano, Wisconsin, has provided the best example and the best hope. Wisconsin has tightly restricted sturgeon fishing since 1903, and Lake Winnebago now has the only large, self-sustaining sturgeon population in the world. A long-term program there may provide stocks that will rehabilitate sturgeon in the Great Lakes and throughout Canada.

At the base of the very first rock painting that we visited, a great sturgeon floats above a tiny triangular tent. It is a divining tent, a place where Ojibwe people have always gone to learn the wishes of the spirits and to gain comfort from their teachings. Someday perhaps Kiizhikok's children will find the sturgeon vaulting from the water around Big Island a common sight. I hope so. It was a moment out of time.

Waves

On our way to visit the island and the Eternal Sands, we experience a confluence of shifting winds and waves. Tobasonakwut shows me how the waves are creating underwaves and counterwaves. The rough swells from the southeast are bouncing against the rocky shores, which he avoids. The wooded lands and shores will absorb the force of the waves and not send them back out to create confusion. Heading toward open water, we travel behind the farthest island, also a wave cutter. We slice right into the waves when possible. But we are dealing with yesterday's wind, a strong north wind, and swells underneath the waves now proceeding from the wind that shifted, fresh, to the south. I think of what Tobasonakwut's father said, "The creator is the lake and we are the waves on the lake." The image of complexity and shifting mutability of human nature is very clear today. Eventually, we beach our boat at the first little bay. Tobasonakwut starts out, at once, to comb for treasures.

I have the same feeling when I come upon a deserted beach as I do when entering a used bookstore with promisingly messy shelves bearing handwritten signs and directions, or a rummage sale run by beaming white haired people who are handing out free coffee and look like they kept all of their forties soapbox glass dishes and their flowered tablecloths in the original plastic. As I look at the beach, strewn with driftwood and interesting rocks, I have the slightly guilty feeling that I get when I visit the gift shop before the museum. Sure enough, as baby and I beachcomb in the opposite direction from Tobasonakwut, we come across three magnificent eagle spikes, those feathers at the ends of wings, the ones used by sun dancers in their sage crowns. But the wind dies suddenly at the margin of the beach and we are edged from the fabulous pickings by biting blackflies and the big droning horseflies that drive moose insane. To avoid the flies, the baby and I take to water just like the moose do.

I plop down and let the waves crash into me at waist height while I nurse the baby. Occasionally her head is spritzed and refreshed. I am wearing a hat, lots of sun-block, dark glasses. The amber-colored water is too rough for leeches to grab onto my legs. I could sit here forever. The pelicans, zhegeg, pass over, twenty or thirty at a time, wheeling in strict formation when up high. Sometimes more casual, they sail down low and I see the boatlike prows of their breasts and drooping gullets. Crowds of black ducks veer over, too. There is a curtain of birds along this beach. Rising and falling, the flocks constantly change and shift. Then, just before me, about seventy feet out, the great fish rears again. This time it hangs even longer in the air, catching sun on its belly, somehow joyous.

"It's all there," Tobasonakwut says upon returning, pointing behind me and then out to the open water.

"What?"

"Atisikan."

The paint that is eternal comes from the Eternal Sands. Just down the beach the waves have dragged the sand off the tough roots of a low beach plant. The roots are such a brilliant red that from a short distance it looks as though the leaves are bleeding into the water. This is a component of the sacred paint used in the rock paintings. And the fish who showed itself to me is a part of the atisikan too. Sturgeon's oil is one of the bonding agents that will not let go, one of the substances that makes the paint eternal.

Offering

I am almost asleep when I realize that I have seen all that is depicted in the first rock painting, the one that I marveled over, the one that glowed from the rock in all of its complexity. I saw the wild rice, which is the spirit of the wild rice, I saw the bear, I saw the deer, and I saw the nameh. The next morning, we go back to the painting. Tobasonakwut ties up at the base of the rock. I bring a dish of food, including asema, up to the top of the rock. I also leave my favorite ribbon shirt.

It is a leave-taking. I have to tell myself not to look back as we travel away from the rock. It is as though I've left behind something intangible—not the shirt, the tobacco, or the food. It is as though I've written a poem and burned it. Given up a piece of my own spirit. I don't understand the feeling that closes in on me. And even now, as I am writing in my study, and as I am looking at photographs I took of the paintings, I am afflicted with a confusing nostalgia. It is a place that has gripped me. I feel a growing love. Partly, it is that I know it through my baby and through her namesake, but I also had ancestors who lived here generations ago.

The Ojibwe side of my family, who ended up with the surname Gourneau, roamed from Madeline Island in Lake Superior, along what is now the Canadian border, through Lake of the Woods and down to Red Lake, and then out onto the Great Plains and eventually the Turtle Mountains. Baupayakiingikwe, Striped Earth Woman, was one of those ancestors, as was Kwasenchiwin, Acts Like A Boy. Our family was of the Ajijauk or Crane dodem, and the Makwa or Bear dodem. I can't help but imagine that these two women, whose names my mother and sister have searched out of old tribal histories, walked where I've walked, saw what I've seen, perhaps traced these rock paintings. Perhaps even painted them.

Ojibwemowin

My grandfather, Patrick Gourneau, was the last person in our family who spoke his native language, Ojibwemowin, with any fluency. When he went off into the Turtle Mountain woods to pray with his pipe, I stood apart at a short distance, listening and wondering. Growing up in an ordinary small North Dakota town, I thought Ojibwemowin was a language for prayers, like the solemn Latin sung at High Mass. I had no idea that most Ojibwe people on reserves in Canada, and many in Minnesota and Wisconsin, still spoke English as a second language, Ojibwemowin as their first. And then, while visiting Manitoulin Island, Ontario, I sat among a group of laughing elders who spoke only their own language. I went to a café where people around me spoke Ojibwemowin and stood in line at a bank surrounded by Ojibwe speakers. I was hooked, and had to know more. I wanted to get the jokes, to understand the prayers and the *adisookaanug,* the sacred stories, and most of all, Ojibwe irony. As most speakers are now bilingual, the language is spiked with puns on both English and Ojibwemowin, most playing on the oddness of *gichi-mookomaan*, that is "big knife" or American, habits and behavior.

As I was living in New Hampshire at the time, my only recourse was to use a set of Ojibwe language tapes made by Basil Johnson, the distinguished Canadian Ojibwe writer. Unknown to Basil Johnson, he became my friend. His patient Anishinaabe voice reminded me of my grandfather's and of the kindest of elders. Basil and I conversed in the isolation of my car as I dropped off and picked up children, bought groceries, navigated tangled New England roads. I carried my tapes everywhere I went. The language bit deep into my heart, but I could only go so long talking with Basil on a tape. I longed for real community. At last, when I moved to Minnesota, I met fellow Ojibwe people who were embarked on what seems at times a quixotic enterprise—learning one of the toughest languages ever invented.

Ojibwemowin is, in fact, entered in the Guinness Book of World Records as one of the most difficult languages to learn. The great hurdle to learning resides in the manifold use of verbs—a stammer-inducing complex. Ojibwemowin is a language of action, which makes sense to me. The Ojibwe have never been all that materialistic, and from the beginning they were always on the move. How many things, nouns, could anyone carry around? Ojibwemowin is also a language of human relationships. Two-thirds of the words are verbs, and for *each verb*, there can be as many as six thousand forms. This sounds impossible, until you realize that the verb forms not only have to do with the relationships among the people conducting the action, but the precise way the action is conducted and even under what physical conditions. The blizzard of verb forms makes it an adaptive and powerfully precise language. There are lots of verbs for exactly how people shift position. *Miinoshin* describes how someone turns this way and that until ready to make a determined move, *iskwishin* how a person behaves when tired of one position and looking for one more comfortable. The best speakers are the most inventive, and come up with new words all of the time. *Mookegidaazo* describes the way a baby looks when outrage is building and coming to the surface where it will result in a thunderous squawl. There is a verb for the way a raven opens and shuts its claws in the cold and a verb for what would happen if a man fell off a motorcycle with a pipe in his mouth and drove the stem of it through the back of his head. There can be a verb for anything.

Tobasonakwut delights in the language, his first language. He loves to delineate the sources and origins of words, keeps lists of new words, and creates them himself. Yet, as with many of his generation, he endured tremendous punishment for this love. He remembers singing his father's song to comfort himself as he was driven to a residential school at age eleven. The priest who was driving stopped the car, made him get out, and savagely beat him. Tobasonakwut spoke no English when he first went to school and although he now speaks like an Ivy League professor if he wants to, he stubbornly kept his Ojibwemowin. Tobasonakwut says that the beatings and humiliations only made him the fiercer in loving and preserving his language. As he says this he clutches his heart, as if the language is lodged there. From the beginning, even as a child, he determined that he would speak it as often as he could.

For Tobasonakwut, Ojibwemowin is the primary language of philosophy, and also of emotions. Shades of feeling can be mixed like paints. *Kawiin gego omaa ayasinoon*, a phrase used when describing loneliness, carries the additional meaning of missing a part of one's own being. Ojibwe is especially good at describing intellectual and dream states. One of Tobasonakwut's favorite phrases is *andopawatchigan*, which means "seek your dream," but is lots more complicated. It means that first you have to find and identify your dream, often through fasting, and then that you also must carry out exactly what your dream tells you to do in each detail. And then the philosophy comes in, for by doing this repeatedly you will gradually come into a balanced relationship with all of life.

My experience with the language is of course very different. Instead of the language being beaten out of me, I've tried for years to acquire it. But how do I go back to a language I never had? I love my first language—why complicate my life with another? I will never have the facility to really use the flexible descriptive power of this language. Still, I love it. The sound comforts me. I feel as though all along this language was waiting for me with kindness. I imagine God hears this language. Perhaps my grandfather's use of the language penetrated. What the Ojibwe call the *Gizhe Manidoo,* the ineffable and compassionate spirit residing in all that lives, is associated for me with the flow of Ojibwemowin. My Catholic training touched me intellectually and symbolically, but apparently never engaged my heart.

Ojibwemowin is one of the few surviving languages that evolved to the present here in North America. For an American writer, it seems crucial to at least have a passing familiarity with the language, which is adapted to the land as no other language can possibly be. Its philosophy is bound up in northern earth, lakes, rivers, forests, and plains. Its origins pertain to the animals and their particular habits, to the shades of meaning in the very placement of stones. Many of the names and songs associated with these places were revealed to people in dreams and songs—it is a language that most directly reflects a human involvement with the spirit of the land itself. It is the language of the paintings that seem to glow from within the rocks.

That is not to say Ojibwemowin is an elevated language of vanished spirituality. One of my favorite words is *wiindibaanens* or computer. It means "little brain machine." Ojibwe people have words for animals from other continents. *Genwaabiigigwed,* the long-necked horse, is a giraffe. *Ojaanzhingwedeyshkanaad,* rhinoceros, the one with the horn sticking out of his nose. *Nandookomeshiinh* is the lice hunter, the monkey. There are words for the serenity prayer used in twelve-step programs and translations of nursery rhymes. The varieties of people other than Ojibwe or Anishinabe are also named: *Aniibiishaabookewininiwag,* the tea people, are Asian. All Europeans are *Omakakiiininiwag,* or frog people, but the French are *Wemitigoozhiwag,* the wooden-cross people. Catholics, who included the Jesuit priests, are *Mekadewikonayewininiwag,* the black-robe men. *Agongosininiwag,* the chipmunk people, are Scandinavian. I'm still trying to find out why.

When it comes to nouns, there are blessedly fewer of them and no designations of gender, no feminine or masculine possessives or articles. Nouns are mainly designated as animate or inanimate, though what is alive and dead doesn't correspond at all to what an English speaker might imagine. For instance, the word for stone, *asin,* is animate. After all, the preexistence of the world according to Ojibwe religion consisted of a conversation between stones. People speak to and thank the stones in the sweat lodge, where the asiniig are superheated and used for healing. They are addressed as grandmothers and grandfathers. Once I began to think of stones as animate, I started to wonder whether I was picking up a stone or it was putting itself into my hand. Stones are no longer the same as they were to me in English.

Ojibwemowin was of course a language of memory, an oral language, passed on by community but not written. For most of the last two centuries, missionized students adapted the English alphabet and wrote phonetically.

Ojibwe orthography has recently been standardized so that the language can be taught in schools and universities. In this book, I have tried to use mainly accepted spellings, although I've fudged a little with Ojibwe words that might be confused with English words, and done my best on words that aren't in the *Concise Dictionary of Minnesota Ojibwe,* by Nichols and Nyholm. I've mastered shamefully little of the language. I'm still working on its most basic forms. Even if I do occasionally get a sentence right, there are so many dialects of Ojibwe that, for many speakers, I'll still have gotten it wrong. And yet, as ludicrous as my Ojibwe must sound to a fluent speaker, I have never, ever, been greeted with a moment of impatience or laughter. Perhaps people wait until I've left the room, but more likely, I think, there is an urgency about attempting to speak the language.

To native speakers like Tobasonakwut, the language is a deeply loved entity. A spirit or an originating genius belongs to each word. Before attempting to speak this language, students petition these spirits with gifts of cloth, tobacco, and food. Anyone who attempts Ojibwemowin is engaged in something more than learning tongue twisters. However awkward my nouns, unstable my verbs, however stumbling my delivery, to engage in the language is to engage the spirit of the words. And as the words are everything around us, and all that we are, learning Ojibwemowin is a lifetime pursuit that might be described as living a religion.

Gigaa-waabamin

Ojibwe people don't say good-bye, that's too final. "I'll see you" is as close to good-bye as the language goes for a common parting. Some habits of Ojibwe have filtered into my English and I find that I can't say good-bye, or if I do, I have to soften it with see-you-laters and have-funs and always, to my children and Tobasonakwut, drive-carefully. *Weweni,* careful. Or, as others jokingly say, *weweni baba-manadis,* which translates roughly as an admonition to be careful as you go around being ugly in your ugly life. Or *gego anooj igo ezhichigeken.* Don't do any of the weird things that I would. *Gigaa-waabamin* means "I'll see you again." That's just the way it is. He has a complicated life up north and I have a complicated life down in Minneapolis, so there is a lot of gigaa-waabamin.

CHAPTER FOUR

Books

The Skylark Motel

Weary, Kiizhikok and I stop at a spot just off the highway,
one of those square tubes of rooms facing the road. The
line of identical brown doors and windows, like staring
faces, has a sullen aspect. No skylarks. The texturized sid-
ing is a defeated looking tan color. There is a small office,
dim but for a glowing television screen. The yard is dust,
struggling weeds, trampled gravel. When looking for a
small motel, I usually choose a place with window boxes,
or at least a few flowers growing in a tractor tire filled
with dirt, feeling hope rise at that small signal of care.
But it's late, Kiizhikok is hungry, and I'm disoriented,

as one always is leaving some wild place on the Earth and returning to human disorder. The unattractive nature of the towns and buildings seems purposeful. There is a belligerent streak to the ugliness. Or maybe I'm just tired. Here is an island, but of a very different sort.

The loneliness of roadside motels steals over me at once. Walking into my room, number 33, even with Kiizhikok's presence to cushion me, the sadness soaks up through my feet. True, I might have dreams here, these places always inspire uneasy nights and sometimes spectacular and even numinous dreams. But they test my optimism. My thoughts go dreary. The door shows signs of having been forced open. I can still see the crowbar marks where a lock was jimmied. And oh dear, it is only replaced with a push-in knob that can be undone with a library card, or any stiff bit of plastic, I think, as I don't suppose that someone intent on breaking into room 33 would use a library card. Or if they did, I wonder, dragging in one duffle and the diaper bag, plus Kiizhikok football-style, would it be a good sign or a bad sign? Would it be better to confront an ill-motived intruder who was well read, or one indifferent to literature?

I rein my thoughts in, get my bearings. There are touches. Although the bed sags and the pickle-green coverlet is pilly and suspicious looking, the transparent sheets are tight and clean. A strangely evocative fall foliage scene is set above the bed—hand painted! Signed with a jerky black squiggle. The bathroom shower has a paper sanitary mat picturing a perky mermaid, breasts hidden by coils of green hair. The terrifying stain in the center of the carpet is almost covered with a woven rug. As always, on car trips where I will surely encounter questionable bedcovers, I've brought my own quilt. There is a bedside lamp with a sixty-watt bulb, and once Kiizhikok is asleep I can read.

Reading Sebald's *Austerlitz* in a cheap motel, insecure, with a chair pushed beneath the doorknob and the drapes held shut with hair clips, is an experience for which I will always be grateful. Books. Why? For just such a situation. Marooned in this uneasy night, shaken by the periodic shudder of passing semi trucks, every sentence grips me. My brain holds onto each trailing line as though grasping a black rope in a threatening fog. I finish half a page, then read it over again, then read the next half of the page and then the entire page, twice. Not many books can be read with such intimacy, nor are there many so beautifully composed that the writing alone brings comfort. I carry *Middlemarch* along with me on book tours because the elaborate twists in George Eliot's sentences provoke in me a mood of concentrated calm.

Austerlitz is about the near dissolution of a man's personality during the reconstruction of his memory. Austerlitz, who has forgotten most of his early childhood, follows threads of history, traceries of his own consciousness; he digs through lists of deportees and examines photographs and propaganda movies to find the truth of his origins. He learns that he was sent on a children's transport from Prague to England at the beginning of World War II, and that his mother died in the humanly mechanized and phenomenally cruel "model ghetto" of Theresienstadt. He understands this slowly. The book moves minutely along this path toward knowledge, and seems at every sentence to deviate but always returns to the unfolding story. It is a very simple book, and unbearably profound. Page after page is about how history sinks into the mind, tormentingly sometimes, and what arrests and disturbances truth causes until finally the human heart can accept its sorrows, heal itself by enduring the unendurable, and go on beating.

The books we bring to strange places become guides and prevailing metaphors, catch-alls, lenses for new experience. As I read late into the night, moths whirling at the spotted shade, this book speaks to me with melancholy prescience, anticipating 9/11 in the first pages when Austerlitz speaks of how the smallest buildings—cottages, little pavilions—bring us peace, while we contemplate vast buildings, overdone buildings, with a wonder which is also dawning horror "for somehow we know by instinct that outsize buildings cast the shadow of their own destruction before them, and are designed from the first with an eye to their later existence as ruins." The description of the village of Llanwddyn, in Wales, submerged by the waters of a great reservoir, reminds me of the sensations I experience when talking to Tobasonakwut about the many settlements and cabins far out on Lake of the Woods, some of them drowned. Like Austerlitz, I too feel as though I've seen the vanished people walking, felt their eyes upon me, and that when I stare down into the opaque water, they are somehow calmly looking up from their ordinary tasks, which they have carried on, below us, for thousands of years.

I try to stay awake for as long as I can, getting up to wash my face at the rust-stained sink. Every time I turn on the tap unseen pipes clunk. Finally, one page sluices into the next and I start awake to find I have been holding my book upright, perhaps reading in my sleep, for I don't know if my eyes were even shut. And I wonder as I turn out the light and settle into the sagging mattress if my sleeping self understood what it read, and indeed, if I will ever know who I am during these dark hours? Asleep, we are strangers to ourselves. Sometimes, as now, it seems odd that we go on day after day accepting this great dislocation, growing used to it, trusting that our night self resembles our day self, that neither will betray the other come morning.

Kay-Nah-Whi-Wah-Nung

On Minn. 11 driving east toward the border crossing at International Falls, I see a large billboard that advertises "a gathering place of historical interest." Kah-Nah-Whi-Wah-Nung. I'm intrigued and as I have some time to dispose of, I decide to investigate. The road I am directed down is quite deserted, and for many miles I see only pastures, a few tawny brown cows, fence posts and gravel. Then suddenly I turn into a large parking lot filled with cars from as far away as Illinois and Florida. The place is still mysterious. From the lot I can see only a wooden door and part of a cedar shake roof. Upon entering the door, and facing a sudden and surprising curve of descending stairs, I understand I've come upon some sort of museum. As I walk down the long, wide, yellow stone staircase, the building opens into a cool, graceful, pleasant interior space divided into display sections, a book and craft shop, and an aquarium filled with live sturgeon, *namewag*.

I'm very glad to see the sturgeon close up, and watch them eagerly. They are, indeed, strangely ancient-looking with their rumpled snouts and whiskers. Their bellies are a cool off-white and their skins are gray, the color so soft and they look painted. They are here, in this building, because the Rainy River Band of Ojibwe is raising and releasing them into the Rainy River. These young namewag are the size of large walleyes, but they may grow to be underwater giants, like the one that Kiizhikok and I saw at the Eternal Sands, or even bigger.

After looking through the displays of Ojibwe life and at the collections of artifacts, I treat myself to the gift shop. I find a number of handmade mocassins, the word is from the Ojibwe, usually spelled *makazinan.* These locally made makazinan are unusually fine, some made with brain-tanned moosehide, No. 13 beads or cut beads, and lined with blanket material or rabbit fur. I pick out several pairs, and then find a book of poems, *Spirit Horses,* by an Ojibwe poet I admire named Al Hunter. The woman who handles the sale proudly tells me that she's Al's niece, and that he happens to be downstairs.

I point out my name on the back cover of Al's book, a blurb. Al comes upstairs and we sit down in the little café which serves fresh, beautiful, Ojibwe-influenced wild rice soups, casseroles, fruit salads. We drink the ubiquitous iced tea of this part of Canada. Al and his partner Sandra recently completed a walk around Lake Superior to draw attention to its pollution. That's a long walk. Al says the days merged, and that time was beautiful. He works for his band, Rainy River Ojibwe, on a land claim that has had promising results—so far, this center, which is located on land containing huge burial mounds restored to the tribe, is one of those results. He tells me something very striking. He says that when he returned home after his education, to work, there were many terrible and pressing needs to address on his reserve—poverty, alcoholism, despair—so he called a meeting. At this meeting, he needed to tell people there was something that their reserve gravely needed. A library.

Books. Why?

Because they are wealth, sobriety, and hope.

Al's reserve now has a library bought with tribal contributions and slowly filling with books.

The Border Crossing

I try not to be nervous, but I can't help it—I am carrying those eagle spikes and although I have a right to carry them and I have my band enrollment card, I hate the questioning, the scrutiny, the suspicious nature of the border guards. What I don't expect is that the man, my age, very trim and professional looking in his blue uniform, will question me about my baby.

"Do you have any proof that you're her mother?"

I stare at him in shock, it is such a strange question. I have to think.

"Well," I say, "I can nurse her."

He stares back at me. Gestures to the side of a building. "Pull over."

Am I going to be required to nurse my baby in front of some border-crossing guard? I pull over, wishing that I had a copy of the Jay Treaty, which guarantees Native People the right to cross the Canadian–U.S. border without hassle. A woman meets me. I undergo more questioning. I start to grip Kiizhikok a little harder, in alarm I suppose, and in response she holds onto me tightly. The guard asks a series of easy questions and then, suddenly, as though to trip me up, shoots the question, "And who is this?" at me, indicating Kiizhikok. Each time, grasping the strategy, I shoot right back, "My daughter!" Each time, Kiizhikok grips me even tighter. I'm so glad she isn't going through one of those mother-rejecting stages, or branching out adventurously, or growling at me, as she likes to do as a joke, right now. Eventually, the sharp-eyed woman clears us. We've passed some mother/daughter test. But when I get into the van I find that I'm actually shaken. For the first time in quite a while I'm surprised to find that I crave a stiff drink. Yes, I do. A straight shot of really good whiskey. And a cigarette.

"What have they done to me?" I say out loud, buckling her in, giving her the baby cell phone *and* the Chinese blender *and* her sippy cup, then buckling myself in and guzzling water from a plastic bottle. It's time to get out of International Falls and back onto a lake.

Meeting Up Again

Once again there is this meeting-up uncertainty. I am supposed to rendezvous with members of the Lac Court Oreilles Ojibwe Language Society. We are going to stay together at an island on Rainy Lake among Ernest Oberholtzer's thousands of books. There was a phone call, a plan, a lost cell phone number, a time to meet. The words Super Stop or Stop and Super or One Stop or Super Shop and Save. Immediately after hanging up I should have written down the name of the meeting place! As I enter International Falls I am more and more confused by the similarity of gas station stop names and supermarkets. They seem to have the same name in various combinations.

I make a slow examination of each one, but don't find my friends. Finally, I haul Kiizhikok out and we do a magnificent shopping at a place called Super One. We buy fresh cherries and all the makings for a corn stew and for an innovative type of trail mix that we have developed on this trip—one that includes salted nuts, pecans, figs, cinnamon chips, and golden raisins. We buy milk, lettuce, and a box of arrowroot baby crackers. Slowly, we walk the aisles, waiting for our friends, until I realize that in one-half hour I have to meet the boat that will take us out to the island.

As it turns out, it was just lateness, an Ojibwe trait so common it is not considered a failing. I'm relieved to see that everyone is gathering and consolidating gear once I go out to the point from which we will embark. My particular friends are a young couple with a baby boy just Kiizhikok's age. They are Ojibwe teachers and very passionate about the language. They speak only Ojibwe to their son, and to my baby, too. She understands them and has quite a few Ojibwe words. Her shoes are *maki* for makizanan and her water is *nibi,* but we have a long way to go before sentence structure. We are going to drive out in a pontoon boat steered by the caretaker of the island, a very agreeable, sunny-haired woman from Ames, Iowa, named Mary Holmes.

Years ago, Mary fell in love with the island of the books, became a caretaker of that island, and is now on the board of the small foundation that administers a tiny trust and takes care of the estate that belonged to Ernest Oberholtzer. The trust allows a few small groups to visit the ecologically fragile island. Because Ernest Oberholtzer was a close friend to the Ojibwe, the foundation honors that relationship by allowing teachers and serious students of the language, as well as one or two Ojibwe writers, to visit on retreats. Most people who come to Ober's island more than a few times become working members of the loose conglomerate of people who support the place in one way or another. It is the kind of place that inspires a certain energy that I can only term "Oberholtzerian"—a combination of erudition, conservationism, nativism, and exuberant eccentricity. Perhaps, I think, the air of Tinkertoy idealism here has something to do with the confluence of fascinations that occurs when Germans and Ojibwe people mix. This place reminds me quite a bit of my own family.

Ernest Oberholtzer

He was born in 1884, grew up in an upper middle-class home in Davenport, Iowa, suffered a bout of rheumatic fever that weakened his heart. He went to Harvard, where he made friends with bookish people like Conrad Aiken and Samuel Eliot Morison. His heart kept bothering him. Told by a doctor he had just one year to live, he decided to spend it in a canoe. He traveled three thousand miles in a summer. Paddling a canoe around the Rainy Lake watershed and through the Quetico-Superior wilderness was just the thing for his heart, so he kept on paddling. He lived to be ninety-three years old.

Ernest Oberholtzer packed those years with passions and enthusiasms, ceaseless physical activity, and loving friendships. He never married, though he lived on his island with a woman who supported him and apparently would have liked to tie the knot. He was trained to play the classical violin and he loved literature, book collecting, landscape architecture, bike travel, and photographing moose. The greatest political act of his life was to take on the massive lumber companies and save the Boundary Waters, the Quetico-Superior wilderness, I hope for all time. His friendships with the Ojibwe were abiding, he was a devoted and very curious companion. He was attracted to the unknown, to great deeds, and exploration.

In 1912, at the age of twenty-eight, he persuaded an extremely capable fifty-year-old Ojibwe man, Taytahpaswaywitong, Billy Magee, to accompany him on an expedition that he hoped would make his name as an explorer. He intended to travel the Barrens bounded by Lake Winnipeg, Hudson Bay, and Reindeer Lake. The area was unmapped, unknown, unexplored since Samuel Hearne's 1770 expedition. They were, of course, going by canoe.

Oberholtzer wasn't much of a hunter, so they had to pack an inordinate amount of food—seven hundred pounds. Every portage consisted of five round-trips. They had a small window of opportunity before the lakes and rivers would freeze solid, stranding them, and so began their journey in late June. By August they would experience freezing nights and woodlands covered in frost. By September, October, and at last November, they would be paddling for their lives. Filling in blanks on the map by using a compass and watch that his mother had given him, Ober mapped the terrain through which they passed. They paddled steadily, and thereby estimated distances hour by hour. Often lost, they desperately navigated mazey lakes, ultimately Nueltin, or Sleeping Island Lake, searching for a river called Thiewiaza that would deliver them in a path toward Hudson Bay.

Loneliness, anxiety, and the strangeness of the lake itself worked on Oberholtzer and at times his journal entries took on a desperate, dreamy quality. On the Barrens, the men hallucinated, lost themselves, but managed to plunge on. Ober saw trees as city smokestacks, people who weren't there. Ever after, the journey was to haunt Ober and remain mysterious to others. At one point he climbed an esker and left in a can a note with his last words. In his journal, Ober notes that Billy Magee would tell him how, every night, he talked in his sleep or made horrible noises. The two came down the side of Hudson Bay. They missed the last steamer out of the country to run before the lakes and rivers froze over, and so they headed south just a hair before winter, freezing all the way and paddling fourteen hours at a stretch, often through the night, their feet and legs stuffed all around with wild hay. Incredibly, they paddled until the first week of November, through snow, along the shore of Lake Winnipeg, and at last made the small settlement of Gimli, Manitoba. There, the two beached their canoe, got haircuts, and returned to the world. They had been paddling and portaging non-stop, often deep into the night, since June 25.

It was a grueling, original, life-changing feat. Though Ober lectured on the trip, he never managed to write about it. Joe Paddock observes in *Keeper of the Wild:*

> Though a conflicted desire to do so haunted him into old age, Ober would never publish or even complete a written account of the Hudson Bay trip. Over the years, whenever he did try to write of it he was overwhelmed with emotion. One is reminded of Meriwether Lewis's inability to write of his great wilderness adventure. As with Lewis, Ober's careful journal of the trip may in itself be the significant book he hoped would one day tell his tale.

That book, *Toward Magnetic North,* has recently been published along with many of the extraordinary photographs that Ober took of the places and of the people he encountered. His photographs of a family of Inuit hunters who took them in and guided them at the northernmost reach of their voyage are the most remarkable. In one, an ancient woman, probably about my age, is framed by a huge stack of wood on her back. She drags herself along or rights herself with two sticks. Another, of a ten-year-old boy to whom his father gave the pipe Ober offered the family as a gift, smokes that pipe gazing with shrewd and thoughtful economy into a familiar distance.

Ober's House and Ober's Books

On reaching the island, I find I am the last to choose a place to stay. I'm thrilled to find that no one else has decided to sleep at Oberholtzer's house. Though each cabin has its own charm, I've always wanted to stay at Oberholtzer's. I want to stay among what I imagine must have been his favorite books. The foundation has tried to keep the feeling of Ober's world intact, and so the books that line the walls of his loft bedroom were pretty much the ones he chose to keep there, just hundreds out of more than 11,000 on the island. Heavy on Keats, I notice right off, as we enter. Volumes of both the poems and letters. Lots of Shakespeare. A gorgeously illustrated copy of *Leaves of Grass*. In some shelves in an alcove above the bed, curious volumes on sexuality including Kraft-Ebbing. I take down one work entitled *Sin and Sex,* and find that an old letter has been used as a bookmark. I read the letter, which is from Oberholtzer to his mother. The subject of the letter is the stock market. Oh well. I replace the letter in the book. Kiizhikok and I spread our quilts on the bed and then we lay down to admire the view from the bed, straight down a rocky channel into a lovely little bay.

Both of the islands next to this one, also owned by the foundation, are kept wild. This island, Mallard, is planted with cheerful care—pink petunias in bark planters. Baskets of salmon impatiens. Tiny perennial gardens of daisies and lilies are set against stone walls. It has seven cabins and two outhouses. But to call the buildings cabins and the privies outhouses is completely inadequate. To start with, Oberholtzer's house is built against the side of a rock and rises three full stories with a surprise sleeping cupola on top, a secret room that can be reached only through a ladder leading into what looks like a chimney. For handles, the sturdy riveted doors are fitted with pieces of curved driftwood, or antlers. The very first floor, the kitchen, is reached either through a trapdoor from above, or an outside screen door above stone steps that lead directly down into the lake. Next to the kitchen door, against the cool of another rock wall, an ice house is set, disguised by vines that loop over a pale turquoise door. I love this door-leading-into-the-stone-hill. I have photographed it many times. There is a Japanese teahouse at the end of the island. To reach it, one crosses an arched stone bridge. Another set of stone steps leads into what is called The Roman Bath—a deep tub of silky lake. There is The Birdhouse, rising like a

Seuss concoction into the pines, story after story, with a zigzag of steps and ladders. As the other cabins are, it's heated with a tiny woodstove. There is one more house, made like the others of unpeeled cedar logs, there is a library cabin, which I'll get to, and there are the outhouses. Mine is built with a tiny step up, a perfect screen door, a lovely window, and a long view down the center of the channel facing east.

We convene to eat in an old early twentieth-century cook's barge used by lumber companies to feed their crews as they ravaged the northern old-growth trees and floated the logs down to the sawmills. Ober had this cook's barge hauled onto his island. An old bell signals meals. Original plates and dishes of every charm—Depression glass, milk glass, porcelains, and sweet old flowery unmatched Royal Doulton china dishes—crowd the open shelves. A cabin just out front of the cook's barge, hauled here too, was once a floating whorehouse, I am told. Now it houses a piano, and three neat beds. A child has written a sign, tacked to its wall, that advises visitors not to be alarmed if they see things they are unprepared to see—like spirits. There is supposed to be a spirit family that inhabits this island.

I'll tell you right off, I don't see hide nor hair of the spirits. But I can't speak for Kiizhikok, with her still open fontanel. They might be talking to her. Or singing her to sleep. Because she sleeps on this island, takes naps of an unprecedented length and then tumbles into sleep beside me as I read long into the night. There is a fever that overcomes a book-lover who has limited time to spend on Ober's island. A fever to read. Or at least to open the books. There is no question of finishing or even delving deeply. I have only days. Among the books, I feel what is almost a low swell of grief, a panic.

Once the baby is asleep I vault to Ober's shelves. I first wash and dry my hands—I just have to. Really, I suppose I should be wearing gloves. Then with a kind of bingeing greed I start, taking one book off the shelf, sucking what I can of it in, replacing it. This goes on for as many hours as I can stand. G. K. Chesterton on William Blake. *Ben Jonson's Works in Four Volumes,* Oxford University, 1811. *Where The Blue Begins* by Christopher Morley, illustrated by Arthur Rackham, first edition and first printing. An 1851 copy of *The House of the Seven Gables.* And *The Voyages of Peter Esprit Radisson, Being an Account of His Travels and Experiences Among the North American Indians.* A wonderful volume, more recent than most, published in 1943 and transcribed from original manuscripts in the British Museum. I keep reading this last book until, late at night, the loons in full cry, my mosquito coil threading citronella smoke, I have to quit. Knowing that I must be alert enough tomorrow to feed Kiizhikok and take the stones from her mouth, I force myself to sleep. But as I drift away with her foot in my hand I am led to picture an alternate life.

In my imagined life, there is an enchanted interlude. All children are given a year off from school to do nothing but read (I don't know if they'd actually like this, but in my fantasy my daughters are exquisitely happy). We come to this island. One year is given to me, also, to read. I am not allowed to write. I am forced to do nothing but absorb Oberholtzer's books. Every day, I pluck down stacks of books from the shelves upon shelves tacked up on every wall and level of each of the seven cabins on Ober's island. Slowly, I go through the stacks, reading here and there until I find the book of which I must read every word. Then I do read every word, beneath a very bright lamp. When my brain is stuffed my daughters and I go swimming, play poker, or eat. Life consists of nothing else.

Ober and Moose

I find some lovely photographs of moose among the archives—Oberholtzer took them. Tracking down, sneaking up on, and photographing moose was a big passion with him. His guide, companion, and mentor, Billy Magee or Taytahpaswaywitong, thought Ober just a little strange, but went along with it, bringing him to within feet of some of the shiest and orneriest creatures of the lake. The photographs that resulted were the first such ever taken of the animal, and Oberholtzer became known as a great expert. *Keeper of the Wild* makes use of notes that Ober took on those photography trips. I think, of course, of the three young female moose we saw in Lake of the Woods, those awkward young beauties cavorting in the reeds, and so innocent about our approach. Ober wrote beautifully about a similarly trusting young bull:

Inch by inch, scarcely moving, Billy propelled the canoe forward, while I knelt in the bow, camera in hand. The sun was fiercely hot, there was only a breath of breeze. The little bull several times raised his head to gaze at us wonderingly; and each time Billy stopped paddling. Thus, during the moments when the moose's head was submerged, we advanced till we were only twenty feet away. The bull edged off a foot or so, turned his back, and suddenly faced around again, whined ever so slightly like a dog and at last, after a moment's reflection, dipped his head under water. I was itching to take his picture, but I noticed something remarkable. Instead of immersing his head completely, as is the custom of the moose when feeding, he left half his long ears protruding. He was *listening;* and I was afraid that, if I clicked the shutter, he would scamper away. When he raised his head again, however, I decided to chance it. I clicked. He flinched, moved away a step again and then resumed his feeding. He seemed completely reassured, for I noticed now that even the tips of his ears were under water. We were still gliding nearer. I took another picture, a third, one after another. At last, lo and behold, the little fellow got down on his knees on the river bottom, and for a second or so his body was wholly lost to sight. His head came up first, with ears pricked. He shook it and the ears flapped drolly against his cheeks. When he rose, he looked at us inquiringly, almost mischievously, with his languid brown eyes. His shaggy winter coat was still clinging in patches to his hindquarters.... To my great surprise he calmly stepped toward us and sniffed with his long snout; and I could have touched him with the paddle. But Billy, always cautious and respectful toward a moose, backed the canoe a few strokes. Thus for fifteen minutes we played with this strange neighbor.

Feasting

The blueberries, *miinan,* have ripened on the island. The first thing Kiizhikok does the next morning is crouch low to the berry bushes and stuff herself with miinan. I show her how. This is the one traditional Ojibwe pursuit I'm good at. Now, before Kiizhikok picks and eats all of the blueberries, it is time to feast the first ripening. Rose Tainter, a traditional elder from Lac Court Oreilles, prays in Ojibwemowin, with her sacred pipe, at breakfast. We have a huge bowl of blueberries. A spirit dish is prepared. The dish is made up of small portions of the food we'll eat, with tobacco set alongside the portions. The spirit dish is either left outside for the spirits or burned as an offering. This is the way the Ojibwe have always given thanks for the first berries of the year. After Rose has finished praying and the spirit dish is set outside, we eat. We eat seriously. We eat with attention. We eat with a lot of laughing.

It seems to me that Ojibwe people always eat with happy grace. Food is part of every gathering and ceremony. Even our weekly meetings to learn the language are based around a potluck dinner, mainly centered around casseroles heavy on wild rice. Today on Ober's island, breakfast consists of pancakes and Ojibwe maple syrup,

scrambled eggs, fresh walleye breaded and fried, a hash of potatoes and crisp turnips, and a big bowl of blueberries. There is also lots more fruit on the side, coffee, and black tea. We'll have a big lunch just a couple hours after the breakfast dishes are cleared and washed. And then dinner, which might involve venison sausage, more walleye, boiled cabbage and potatoes, or if we are lucky enough to see Nancy Jones, whatever she has hunted might appear.

Nancy Jones, Ogimaawigwanebiik, happens to be one of the most extraordinary women I know.

For starters, she holds the world record as the quickest beaver skinner. I don't know where, exactly, she earned the World's Quickest Beaver Skinner title, but I'm assured this is the truth. She makes a few judicious cuts and turns the animal inside out. It's like sleight of hand. Nancy does exquisite beadwork, placing each tiny cut bead just so on makazinan of smoked moosehide, trimmed with otter fur, lined with blanket. Nancy has a great laugh and deep spiritual knowledge, she is an Ojibwe language teacher, and fiercely devoted to Ojibwe culture. Her children are language teachers, too, and she has taught them her bush skills. Still, they are amazed at her fortitude and endurance. Nancy has been known to kill, skin, and cart back to her cabin a whole moose *and* a deer in one day. She can snare rabbits, trap anything from lynx to pine marten. She can shoot the head off a partridge sitting in a tree, and probably catch the partridge as it falls, too. Ojibwe are meat eaters, that's just how it is. The joke goes: What is an Ojibwe vegetarian called? A poor hunter. Nevertheless, it was Nancy's deer haunch and a fat string of bass three years ago that changed my then youngest daughter, Aza, from a supermarket carnivore to a thoughtful vegetarian.

It was either the deer haunches, or the ribs. Anyway, on our last visit to Ober's island, Aza made a decision from which she has never deviated. I was amazed that a ten-year-old could decide with such conviction. She won't even eat a fish after she went to the dock to check on Nancy's stringer. Later, she said to me that one of the fish had looked up at her. That did it. I must have been a hard-hearted little person, because as the granddaughter of a pair of butchers I helped kill chickens and watched from a corner of the slaughterhouse as my uncle knocked sheep, shot cows, scalded and gutted dead pigs. And yet it has taken my daughter Aza to make me really attempt anything like a consistently vegetarian set of habits, and it started out purely because I felt bound to support her tenderness on behalf of animals.

At any rate, although killing and eating wild game is for the Ojibwe a spiritual as well as delectable enterprise, there is no vegetarianism this year on Ober's island. Nancy and her son Paybomibiness are running an Ojibwe language camp this summer on her land about a forty-five-minute boat ride from Ober's island. They come to stay for a night, but all the game is left at the language camp and so we eat the most incredible spaghetti bolognese. Maybe it's the red pepper flakes in the sauce, or the type of onion.

Maybe it's the air. Maybe it's the mosquitoes, and how we are free of them in the well-screened kitchen.

Nancy remembers Ernest Oberholtzer very well—he made eggs for her family on their first visit, when they paddled over and tied their canoe to his dock. In Oberholtzer's photo archive there are dozens of pictures of Nancy's family, her late husband's family, and of Nancy as a child, strong-minded looking even then, grinning, wearing a soft red woolen hat. Paybomibiness touches a picture on the wall. I recognize it as a photograph of Billy Magee, Taytahpaswaywitong—the man who guided and paddled with Oberholtzer on the great 1912 adventure into the unmapped interior of the Northwest Territories west of Hudson Bay was his grandfather.

Maang

A hot wind blows over the island, and Kiizhikok and I are in and out of the water all afternoon. We edge ourselves carefully down a stone stairway into the cool tea-colored water of Rainy Lake. Pushing off, we float together, into the channel, sighing in dreamy relief. We bob along in our life jackets, talking part Ojibwe, part English, and part mother-baby nonsense. The world is perfect. The shadows are long but on the rocks they still burn like iron. The sun's a fierce gold. Baby and I watch the silhouette of a big loon approach down the channel between islands. It comes nearer and nearer, as silent as we are. Then the *maang* is abnormally close, closer, too close, and again I am filled with the now familiar sense of uneasy assessment. That beak looks sharp! Will it peck Kiizhikok? The loon's eyes are very red! But the loon isn't going to poke my baby, of course, it only circles, coming close enough for us to count the white spots on its back and regard the spectral pupil of its weird reflective eye.

Again, I marvel how animals seem attracted to the baby, and once we have emerged from the water and are drying off in the light breeze, I ask Nancy Jones if she saw the loon swimming with us. I ask modestly, sure that she'll tell me that Kiizhikok has some unusual power to attract maang.

"*Geget,* I saw it," she says casually. "He liked your life jackets."

Our life jackets?

"They're red. That's how we used to catch loons and eat them," Nancy says. "We used red things. They'll come close and investigate anything red." Then she adds, "We don't eat them anymore."

"How did they used to taste?" I ask her.

"Rich," she says.

The Library

I am haunted by a book that I found the first time I visited Ober's island. It was stuck away in a corner of a little cabin I haven't described, one devoted to books alone, the library. My find was a little pamphlet-sized inconsequential-looking book covered with a black paper that looked like oilcloth. I slipped it from the shelf and opened it. *Tristram Shandy*. The first novel in the English language. As it was originally published in serial form this was but a portion of the first edition and first printing. Laurence Sterne had signed the title page. I had a strange, covetous, Golum-like feeling as I held the book, *my precious*. I suppose it was the beginning of the sort of emotional response to books that drives those collectors you hear about, occasionally, to fill their apartments with books until there are only book tunnels to walk through and the floors eventually collapse down onto their neighbors.

Of course, I have to see *Tristram Shandy* again. I want to visit this book, and also to make sure I really saw it. But this time I can't find the book although I crawl with Kiizhikok on hands and knees looking for likely places it could have

been stashed. Its absence bothers me. Although I'm help-
lessly in the grip of other books now, and currently in love
with a corny purple edition of Catlin's journals, I keep
sneaking around the bottom of the shelf where I found my
precious, peeking over other books, behind the shelves, like
a dog sure that it will find a bone hidden years before.

Mary Holmes goes through the catalog with me, and
that particular volume isn't mentioned. Which doesn't
mean, she tells me, that it wasn't actually there. So I might
have seen it. This is, for me, like a birder having possibly

photographed an ivorybill then losing the film. I'm cha-
grined—why didn't I do something about the book? Show
it to someone? Make certain it was cared for? But I know
that the answer is that I didn't because I am in somewhat
uneasy agreement with the spirit of the island, which is to
let the books exist as they were meant to exist, to be read,
to be found and then unfound. To have their own life.
Somehow, that also puts me in conflict with a piece of
my heart. For I also want the books to be protected from
people like me, whose itch to hold them might overwhelm
even the strictest conscience. Even now, I can feel it, the line
is thin. Especially when you can't find *Tristram Shandy*.

   Signed, goddamnit, I'm positive!

   Mary tells me that Ober had left no will regarding the
island and his books and cabins, so that ten years passed
while all of the legalese was sorted out. During those years,
the books were alone. I brood on this. The books. Alone in
the cold and through the humid summers, alone in the
cabins for ten years as roofs collapsed, alone as squirrels
invaded and dismantled eighteenth-century bindings to line
their nests with rare pages. I am afflicted with such melancholy at the thought of the books all alone on the island that
I have to walk back to Ober's house, to nap with Kiizhikok,
to settle my mind. This whole island, filled with books, and
no one to care for them! I would have liked to have been
here. I imagine it as something like living in a great Cornell
Box, only while Joseph Cornell's visual themes were white
spheres and tiny glasses and peeling cubicles and star maps

that suggested vast compressions of time and space, here the themes would be the books, the words stacked endlessly. Spine to spine, margin to margin. Peeling, curling, waiting in a thrilling passivity for someone—like me!

There was an original Edward Curtis portfolio of portraits of American Indians among the books. I'm glad that I don't know what else. Some of the most valuable were sold once the little foundation of Oberholtzer's friends and supporters was formed. In a panic of retrieval, some were bought back. But a piece of the careful intention and depth of Ober's collection was lost. Still, the collection is for me both a caution and an inspiration. It is surely a good thing that Oberholtzer devoted only a portion of his vast energy to book collecting. He was a dedicated bibliophile, careful and disciplined, ordering books from London booksellers with great specificity and detail, and receiving notes and invoices in return, some of which are still tucked into the pages of his books. Nicholas Basbane's wonderful book on book obsession, *A Gentle Madness,* begins with a description of the difference between the bibliophile and the bibliomaniac:

> With thought, patience, and discrimination, book passion becomes the signature of a person's character. When out of control and indulged to excess, it lets loose a fury of bizarre behavior. "The bibliophile is the master of his books, the bibliomaniac their

slave," the German bibliographer Hanns Bohatta steadfastly maintained, though the dividing line can be too blurry to discern. Whatever the involvement, however, every collector inevitably faces the same harsh reality. After years spent in determined pursuit, a moment arrives when the precious volumes must pass to other shelves. Some accept the parting with calm and foresight; others ignore it entirely. Some erect grand repositories as monuments to their taste, others release their treasures with the whispered hope that they reach safe harbor in the next generation.

Whatever Oberholtzer's intentions were, I'm happy that his island is still filled with the books he pursued and acquired. Other than actual writing, the books a person leaves behind reflect most accurately the cast of that person's mind. If his spirit is with the spirit family living on the island, as some believe, then I'm sure that Ober misses his chief treasures, but feels relieved that the collection is more or less intact. For his assemblage does reflect his character, as the best collections do, which is why it is so important that the heart of it be restored. His books on exploration, the great north of Canada and the Arctic, and his painstakingly procured works on Native American life, as well as the volumes of poetry he so loved and the works in German and the books on music, probably reflect as much as anyone can know of him.

Ober and the Ojibwe

One of the reasons, I think, that Ober so loved and was fascinated by the Ojibwe is that he loved the books in the people. He loved the oral tradition of storytelling, where the person becomes the book as in *Fahrenheit 451*. His Ojibwe name, Atisokan, means story. As Paybomibiness tells it, Oberholtzer was always entering a circle of Ojibwe asking eagerly, "Atisokan? Atisokan?" And so, as Ojibwe do, he was affectionately nicknamed. He recorded several stories but never did complete a collection, or indeed, write the books he meant to about the Ojibwe. He hadn't, perhaps, the degree of passivity it takes to actually sit down and write a book. Or he hadn't the patience, maybe, to sit down long at all. His phenomenally active life benefited his Ojibwe friends in many ways, not the least of which is in the area of conservation, and now, in the ongoing hospitality that the board of the Oberholtzer Foundation has shown toward Ojibwe people, Ojibwe writers and language teachers, storytellers. During this retreat to the island, for instance, I am able both to take notes for this book and to work with Keller Paap and

Lisa LaRonge on details of the first book that our nascent publishing house, Birchbark Books, will publish. It is a book by an Ojibwe elder named Nawiigiizis, of Mille Lacs, Minnesota. Ober definitely would have added this book to his collection, and as I leave I promise to send it, and this one, too, up north to the island of books.

CHAPTER FIVE

Home

Telephone

We're going to make the drive straight down to the Cities
without stopping, so I keep Kiizhikok awake throughout
the last morning on the island, until we are on the road.
To keep her eyes open just a little longer, I break out a toy
called Alpha-Bug, who says, "hey, that tickles," when she's
turned on. Press the Alpha-Bug's feet and she says a letter
and can also make the sound of the letter. You can even get
her to say whole words, though not suggestive or swear
words. My older daughters have discovered that Alpha-
Bug won't even say the word "sex." How did they do that?
These toys made with sound chips did not exist when my

other children were young. Kiizhikok happily presses green plastic bug feet until twenty miles south of International Falls, when the letter *D* puts her to sleep.

I have only been in sporadic phone contact with my daughters during this trip, which causes me great anxiety. I know they are fine—as they are teenagers they each have a life project they're embarked on. One is making a film in London, one is studying in the Berkshires, one daughter is part of an international choir. Oddly, it has been easiest to talk to my daughter in London. I sat on a polished log chair at the one radio phone available on Ober's island, and she stood at a phone booth just outside King's College, using a phone card. We compared notes on food. She had found it best to frequent a Greek deli near the school instead of rely on cafeteria sandwiches made of mashed corn and chicken. I had found it best, in Canada, to rely on a trail mix heavy on dried fruit, except of course for the memorable lunch at Kay-Nah-Chi-Wah-Nung and the food shared with Ojibwe food-lovers on Ober's Island.

Now, as I merge just past Cloquet, Minnesota, onto 35 South heading back to Minneapolis, the little cell phone I've taken, silent all along, makes a triumphant tootling sound at the end of its plug-in cord. I start dialing, and talk to my daughters from the road, check in with my household and with my bookstore people, with my sisters and parents. All of a sudden I am back in the web of connection.

I am on the mainland, dry land, off the islands. Or so I think.

Return

We arrive. We return. Home is familiar and it is disorienting. For days, I'm not quite here and not quite there, but muddle around trying to enter the stream of my life. There is a sad discovery. The city forester has painted a blazing red ring and the letter *A,* sign of doom, around Old Stalwart's trunk. This tree is much older than the house, and I've carefully had it treated with a protective fungicide every few years to discourage Dutch Elm disease. The treatment doesn't always work. I knew that. But it's like a friend of mine is stricken. The tree is the classic fluted shape and raises immense and graceful arms high above our three-story house. I love elm trees—grooved bark and sawtooth leaves and fluted silhouette. I think the Earth has chosen to praise the sky by growing this tree.

Even I can see the flags, the stunted and dead leaves, the ailing branches, the signs. I stand outside with the tree, in a state of helplessness—there should be a word specifically for the feeling one has about the death of a tree. I think of photographing Old Stalwart, but I can't bear to. Within days, the city tree crew arrives and saws off those long sweet limbs, lest the disease spread. I'm so sad I cannot look at the tree anymore, it hurts to see it maimed like that. A few more days pass and then the forester seals off the street, notches the rest of the tree, and fells the three-story-high stump onto the asphalt. I watch it go, with Kiizhikok, and feel the shock of its passage, a resounding shudder of the earth that tingles in our feet. That's it. It is gone. This has been a warm winter and a record number of elms have succumbed, as the deep cold helps kill off the beetles that spread the sickness. As I am finishing this book, the city stump grinder arrives and by the end of the day his rotary blade has turned the rest of Old Stalwart into a pile of chips. It will be another hundred years, if the house survives this long, before a tree grown in its place tops the roofline and teases the sky.

Reading Distance

My happiness in being an older mother surprises me— though often worn out I don't seem to mind my sleepy days. I know they quickly pass. Some changes are permanent, though, for instance my middle-aged vision. The first time I held Kiizhikok in my arms, just after she was born, I looked into her perfect face and realized that I couldn't make out her features. I had to adjust her to my reading distance.

It occurs to me, now, that I now do this constantly. If reading is taken to mean comprehending, I step back often. I focus; to my great relief, I have a little more patience. I have learned to appreciate as well as to fear the swift current of hours. Those first jagged months of ceaseless exhaustion passed like dreams, so quickly I feel I've flown in and out of clouds. Already she is making sense of things and I am making sense of her. At the same time, my oldest daughters are soon leaving for college. All this year I have found myself sorting through photographs as though to persuade myself that their childhoods have actually happened, that all of those years really occurred in fabulous particularity.

Returning home, after a long anticipated trip, always does this to me. Time seems foreshortened, furiously spent, a blur. If, as Austerlitz says, time is by far the most artificial of all our inventions, then what am I living in, what is this force that holds me captive in its ineluctable continuance? As I still have *Austerlitz* to finish on my first night home, the book becomes a reassuring messenger from the near past, familiar now, a witness to my travels.

Austerlitz doesn't wear a watch, I am happy to read, considering one "a thoroughly mendacious object." I don't wear a watch either, unless forced by circumstance. He explains what I have never completely thought out about my hope of somehow resisting time through these little forms of protest. Austerlitz hopes, he says, that time will not pass away, has not passed away, that he can turn back and go behind it and there find everything as it once was. I suppose that is the point of sifting through my shoeboxes of photographs. Perhaps that is the point of everything, this writing most of all.

There is a surprise memory for me at the end of *Austerlitz*, one that simultaneously revives a forgotten person, a teacher of mine, and gives me an unexpected metaphor to use in understanding where we have been.

The last pages of the book are about another book, a memoir by Dan Jacobson, a writer whose father, a Lithuanian rabbi, died in 1920 and caused his wife to decide to emigrate with her nine children to South Africa. They were the only people in his family who survived the Holocaust. Jacobson spent most of his childhood in the town of Kimberly, near the diamond mines, which were not fenced off and to the edge of which children ventured to look down into a depth of several thousand feet. As Dan Jacobson was my advisor during what seemed a very long term of study at University College, London, in 1976, I can almost see him describe how it was terrifying to see such emptiness open up a foot away from firm ground, to realize that there was no transition, only this dividing line, with ordinary life on one side and its unimaginable opposite on the other. The chasm into which no ray of light could penetrate, writes the narrator of *Austerlitz,* was Jacobson's image of the vanished past of his family and his people which, as he knows, can never be brought up from those depths again.

Dan Jacobson was a very kind man. I remember that as we talked, perhaps to set me at ease, for I was shy, he used to share chunks of the Cadbury bars he kept in his desk drawer—the kind in the purple wrapper, studded with chunks of nuts and raisins. How odd it seems now that he is with me in Minneapolis, and that I am nodding as I think, yes, it is as though when I look past a generation or into the past of Tobasonakwut's world there is a lightlessness, too, for nine of every ten native people perished of European diseases, leaving only diminished and weakened people to encounter what came next—the aggressions of civilization including government policies and missionaries and residential schools. Yet, here, as I turn to Kiizhikok sprawled in sleep beside me, is a light.

Wood Ticks

A pure little light, I think, reaching over to touch her curls. That is when I find the wood tick. It is still on the move, not attached, which is good. I pluck it away and dispose of it and make certain there are no more. This one was probably carried in on a shirt or blanket. Suddenly, of course, I itch all over. I don't know why they are so much worse than mosquitoes, for instance, but they *are* worse. Or maybe I just have a thing about them. Back on the island while eating lunch with Tobasonakwut, I plucked one off and made a shuddering noise. He opened the top layer of his sandwich and said, "throw him in." When I was a child and visited my grandparents in the Turtle Mountains, we cousins had wood-tick contests at the end of the day, after playing in the woods. Any number under twenty was scorned. I remember one cousin winning one night with a grand total of fifty-six. In the full blush of their season I've seen them swarm toward you off willow branches—swarm slowly. That's what's so awful. Their tiny, blood-drawn, implacable lust.

Up close, they are so small and neatly made. Of course, their true awfulness becomes apparent when they vampirize and grow big. Earlier this summer, about a week after bringing our dog back from a trip up north, Kiizhikok brought me a huge tick she'd found, fallen off the dog. She held it solemnly, pinched carefully between her thumb and first finger, her pinky crooked. Its legs, fine as copper hairs, waved hopelessly. I couldn't breathe for the horror of it—the thing looked like a grape.

Later on I described the moment to Pallas, who was dismissive. "Oh mom," she said, "Kiizhikok's much too intelligent to eat anything with legs that move."

Books. Why?

I've been to the islands and back. I've seen a great many books and held in my hands several that would be set behind glass in the rare books rooms of university libraries. I've touched the rock paintings, and read a fragment of their stories. Part of the trip is always the return, the way it shakes off you, the washing of duffel bags of clothes, the tons of catalogs that have collected in the mailbox. The next day, tick free, but sad over the tree and still disoriented, I walk over to our bookstore, Birchbark Books, in Minneapolis. I started it with my daughters for idealistic reasons—the native community, the neighborhood, the chance to work on something worthy with my girls. But really, in my deepest heart, I wonder now if I started it to cure myself of an affliction of books.

The door is blue because I love blue. It is an old door rescued from the knockdown of some haute bourgeois Minneapolis house. It's beautiful. The window boxes, which I've planted with herbs and flowers, are overflowing now that it's August. And here is one of my favorite people in the world, Mr. Brian Baxter, who manages and oversees the getting and selling of the books at Birchbark Books! Brian, ah Brian, who will read "The Barrel-Organ" or maybe *Mean Soup* or maybe from *The Jungle Book* out loud and with perfect drama. Brian is also afflicted by books, but manages his addiction by having lived and sold books all of his life and by keeping only a small portion, several thousand, of the books that have passed through his hands.

. Our store is pure comfort. Jelly beans, pretzels, and sour cherry bites are free. To create the store, we gutted a dentist's office and brought unpeeled birch trees in to make a loft and birch boards to make floor-to-ceiling shelves. The store has good acoustics. We play our favorites in contemporary native music—from Black Lodge to Carlos Nakai's native flute, and of course Primeaux and Mike's peyote songs, perfect for reading and browsing. This bookstore looks like the inside of a cabin on Ober's island. There is an old Catholic confessional against one wall, bought from a salvage company. There are easy chairs that I've plucked from neighborhood alley dumpsters or boulevards, where they've been

left for the taking. I've had them upholstered in soft denim. I was delighted to walk in one morning to find a writer I much admire sitting in one of these chairs and frowning at the corrections on a final proof of his new book. I am often thrilled when I can sit in the bookstore audience and listen to Susan Power or Jim Northrup read from their work. Writers sign our back wall. Our bathroom is papered with poems. Our office is the former dentist's closet where he prepared fillings and kept dank lunches in a trembling two-foot refrigerator. Now the office/closet is loaded with books and book orders and too many bills to pay, for there is always that, the costliness of any great love.

There is sage, there is sweetgrass, there is red paint. This little bookstore is where I belong and where anyone can belong. It is a home for people who love books and a place that cannot be duplicated by any bookstore corporation—it is just too personal. It is an island, as lovingly itself as any in a lake. In our store, the greedy melancholy that Ober's books inspired falls away. It is an excellent and cheering thing to have a flow of books around you, to see them as they enter, and then take the money from people's hands as they disappear. They must be sold! Taken away! Get thee gone! Still, besides my daily visits, sometimes I come to the store at night. I love to be among the books and to fuss them into pleasant order, just the way I love moving plants around in my garden. One of our booksellers, watching me, says, "Oh, you've come to love the books again?" Being around books is only half about actual reading, after all. The other part is talking about books with other people, a rich topic, and yet another is enjoying their presence. Sitting in the bookstore half-light I feel a great contentment.

Birchbark Books is just off Lake of the Isles. I didn't even think about this before I left, but that's it—the whole thing about islands and books. There really are two islands on Lake of the Isles and they are both wild islands, little places in the city where, from a canoe, I've seen great horned owls, black-crowned night-herons, arctic tern, dozens of black or painted turtles swirling off logs, and once a bald eagle. Maybe I live among the books and islands, and also must visit them in more remote places, because I've decided, in some deeply interior way unavailable to my conscious mind until I've started writing *this* book, that I will order my life to deal with a hoary old cliché.

This cliché has truly nagged at me. It is a question that I've asked myself periodically ever since I was nine years old. The question is: What book would you take to a desert island? I even have the question taped to the top of a cigar box on the bookstore counter, a request to customers to write their favorites on slips of paper, a way to find out about their tastes and discover titles that we've overlooked. What book would you take to a desert island—what a dismal thought! To have only one book to read over and over for years and years. Think of that miserable moment in the movie *Cast Away* when poor Tom Hanks opens a FedEx box and finds a *videocassette*. If only it had been a book! But which book should it have been? My solution is a dictionary. A dictionary would last and last. A dictionary would be a good thing to have arrived in that FedEx box. But even better to be like Oberholtzer and to store up 11,000. Or to be an Ojibwe raised on stories and to contain many books in mind. Or me, with a bookstore.

Books. Why?

So I can talk to other humans without having to meet them.

Fear of boredom.

So that I will never be alone.

Acknowledgments

Tobasonakwut, miigwech, kiizhawenimin. I would also like to thank everyone mentioned in these pages.

To Ojibwe speakers and other experts—I tried my best to get it right and went over it all with Tobasonakwut, but there are probably mistakes that should be corrected. If so, they are mine.

Louise Erdrich is a native of North Dakota, where she was raised by her Ojibwe-French mother and German-American father. She is the author of nine novels, including the National Book Critics Circle Award-winning *Love Medicine* and the National Book Award Finalist *The Last Report on the Miracles at Little No Horse,* as well as poetry and children's books. Her most recent novel, the highly acclaimed *Master Butchers Singing Club,* is a national bestseller. She lives in Minnesota with her four daughters.

This book is set in Garamond 3, designed by
Morris Fuller Benton and Thomas Maitland
Cleland in the 1930s, and Monotype Grotesque,
both released digitally by Adobe.

Printed by R. R. Donnelley and Sons on
Gladfelter 60-pound Thor Offset smooth
white antique paper.

Dust jacket printed by Miken Companies.
Color separation by Quad Graphics.

Three-piece case of Ecological Fiber ivory side
panels with Sierra black book cloth as the spine
fabric. Stamped in Lustrofoil metallic silver.